the great omission

Fulfilling Christ's Commission
Completely

STEVE SAINT

P.O. BOX 55787   SEATTLE, WA 98155

i-tec

10575 SW 147TH CIRCLE
DUNNELLON, FL 34432

YWAM Publishing is the publishing ministry of Youth With A Mission. Youth With A Mission (YWAM) is an international missionary organization of Christians from many denominations dedicated to presenting Jesus Christ to this generation. To this end, YWAM has focused its efforts in three main areas: (1) training and equipping believers for their part in fulfilling the Great Commission (Matthew 28:19), (2) personal evangelism, and (3) mercy ministry (medical and relief work).

For a free catalog of books and materials, contact:

YWAM Publishing
P.O. Box 55787, Seattle, WA 98155
(425) 771-1153 or (800) 922-2143
www.ywampublishing.com

Table of Contents

Dedication
Acknowledgments
Foreword
Endorsements
Introduction

Chapter #1   *What man meant for evil,*
              God meant for good.   15

Chapter #2   *Is this mission impossible?*   37

Chapter #3   *The deception of dependency*   51

Chapter #4   *They do have what it takes!*   69

Chapter #5   *Technology—from prejudice*
              to partnership   85

Chapter #6   *Can stone-age people*
              use space-age technology?   105

Chapter #7   *Money matters more than you know.*   125

Chapter #8   *Are we on the right road?*   142

Chapter #9   *Making poison has its traditions,*
              just like missions.   159

Chapter #10   *Becoming a hero of the faith*   172

Epilogue   191

Dedication

When I was a little boy, God wrote one of the great missionary stories of all time. I had a front row seat because God gave my dad and four of his best friends short but important roles.

Millions of Christians and non-Christians alike have been deeply impacted by this story, but few have ever heard anything about the six other excellent actors who played the villains in the first chapter of the story. I dedicate this book to those six men:

To Nampa – You died before you ever heard that Wangongui (God) wanted to adopt you so that He could take you to live in His place with Him forever. I dedicate this book to you, and I dedicate myself to seeing that as few people as possible die without knowing.

To Guikita – You kept telling me that you wanted to die so that you could go live with my dad whom you speared to death. You kept telling me to stay here to teach the young people in your tribe how to follow God's trail. Well, you got your wish, and I'm doing what you told me to. This book is for you.

To Dyuwi – You killed people as a young man, but when God changed your life, you went on to risk your life to save others. Your love for God's Word is a great example to me. I just wish you could read it for yourself. Your life has made an impact on more people around the world than you even know exist. For your sweet and faithful spirit, this little book is yours.

To Nimonga – I lost touch with you before you died. I don't even know which way you went, but I hope to see you in God's place one day. You played an important role in God's story and never knew it. Not because you were willing, but because you were used by Him for the benefit of others. I would like to dedicate this book to you too.

To Kimo – I know you regret having killed so many people, among them your own wife's family and five missionaries. But as soon as you heard that you could walk God's trail, you were ready and have been faithfully following it ever since. I want to thank you for taking such good care of Star (my Aunt Rachel) until she died. She always appreciated the monkey and wild pig meat that you shared with her. I want to thank you for being my elder and for baptizing me. I too am still walking God's trail!

To Mincaye – Who would have ever believed that after helping kill my children's grandfather, you would end up taking his place? We all love you! Thank you for being my friend and for being willing to take so much time away from your gardens and family to tell foreigners what God has done in your life. You say you lived "badly, badly, hating and killing," but what you meant for evil, God meant for good. Thank you for being willing to put yourself on display in front of thousands of *cowodi* (foreigners). You are an excellent spokesman for God's transforming power. It looks like we get to go on the speaking circuit again. That is why I've written this book. While people are reading it, we'll go get some more of that *ice-keem* you like so much. This book is for you too, Grandfather.

Acknowledgments

One of the reasons it has taken me so long to attempt to write a book is that I have learned from the acknowledgments in other books just how many people it takes to get a book written: wife, parents, children, and a dozen other people.

Authors usually acknowledge people "without whose help the job would never have been completed." Now I realize why those people are acknowledged. I want to acknowledge those same people. You know who you are. Thank you!

This book needed to be written on a "short fuse." I want to especially thank you, Brian Mast, for getting up early and staying up late these last few weeks to make sure the pieces made a whole.

Foreword

I first met Steve and his two friends Mincaye and Tementa when they traveled to Austin to share their story at our church. My heart was so stirred by the beauty of the message and the miracle of God's redemptive plan.

Immediately, God knit our hearts together, and a few months later I had the privilege of traveling with Steve to visit the Waodani in Ecuador. To meet this tribe that has been so gloriously transformed and to walk on the beach where Steve's dad and four friends were killed were experiences that I will never forget.

Steve and I have shared passionately about the strategies and ideas that govern most of the current missionary effort. He is one of the most progressive mission thinkers I know. His love for the world and his sensitivity to the indigenous church is simply inspiring. The ideas revealed in this book will have a profound impact on your life as they have on mine.

There is great hope for reaching every tribe and tongue if we partner with the indigenous believers all around the world with fresh vision and fresh ideas.

For the Kingdom,

Robert J. Koke
Senior Pastor, Shoreline Christian Center
Austin, Texas

About forty years ago, five young men (Nathanael Saint, Jim Elliott, Roger Youderian, Ed McCully, and Peter Fleming) bravely and boldly inspired millions to action. Christ's Great Commission to them was not merely a scripture to be memorized, but a personal mandate to fulfill at any cost.

In that same spirit, the son of one of these bold, brave men picks up the torch in this book. Recently I had the opportunity to be with Steve Saint among the Waodani people in the Amazon jungle. As he shared his strategic insight concerning world missions, my prayer was, "Father, let this insight be shared around the world to multiply effectiveness for Christ's mission. Multiply your work through him as you did through his father's life and death."

To read this book as simply a critique on missions would be a mistake. It is a call to the passion, purpose and purity of Christ-like living. Don't simply read this book to judge its view. Read it to sharpen your sickle for harvest and multiply your effectiveness for world evangelism.

The harvest is great and His laborers are few-we must make our life count!

Jim Graff
Pastor, Faith Family Church
Victoria, Texas

Endorsements

For years, our national recording teams have been able to penetrate areas where language and geographic and cultural barriers often restrict foreign missionary activity. Steve's book clearly underscores the need for this indigenous manpower.

Colin Stott
Executive Director
Gospel Recordings

From a hammock in the Amazon rain forest, we listened intently as Kimo shared his story with our ten-year-old son, Stephen. The realization was instant; we were to learn far more from these amazingly creative people than we could ever hope to teach.

We cannot afford to omit Kimo, and others like him, from fulfilling their role in the Great Commission.

Tim and Janet Solomon,
Missionaries and team leaders of the first Waodani Mission Vision Tour

---

As a professional expedition leader and non-believer, I have spent a surprising amount of time over the past twenty-five years leading U.S. college students to remote locations on the planet, where it is not uncommon for us to meet indigenous Christians.

The Waodani, who in less than four decades have been catapulted through the centuries, are special. They share their light, peace, ingenuity, strength, courage, and unlimited potential with anyone who visits their territory. After spending time with Steve Saint and the Wao people, those students in my groups who may have arrived with a rebellious, non-Christian, anti-missionary stance come away with a new, illuminated point of view.

In this book, Steve shares ideas with you that he has shared with my students. You will find his well-illustrated points enlightening.

Doug Stufflebeam
International Collegiate Expeditions
Mount Vernon, Washington

In recent years, missionaries like myself have expressed concern over the growing confusion in North America about just what missions really is. Good people are spending valuable time and resources doing things that seem productive on the surface but often end up being counter-productive, hurting national churches and ministries instead of helping them.

But how can the average Christian determine if his or her ideas or work are helping or hurting the cause of missions if the people who could tell them don't discuss the issues that make the difference?

In this easy-to-read book, Steve Saint takes a hard look at numerous missions issues rarely addressed and provides humorous illustrations from his own experiences. He offers challenging ideas for how readers can make sure their role is significant in God's great world plan!

Rick Johnson
Missionary to Central and South America

After becoming a Christian in 1975, I encountered the story "Through Gates of Splendor" through various news magazines and in the book by Elisabeth Elliott. At a young age, this story inspired me to actively tell others about Christ regardless of the personal cost.

Twenty years later, through my association with Colin Harbinson (the creator of *Toymaker and Son*) and Wycliffe Bible Translators, I was asked to produce the stage show *Dayuma*, the story of the first Waodani convert. As I saw the impact this moving presentation had on people of all ages, my determination to reach the lost grew even stronger. In 1998 I met Mart Green, the founder and president of Hobby Lobby and Mardels. In this initial meeting, Mart asked me what kind of movie I would want to make. "I would tell the story of Palm Beach and the five missionaries who were martyred by the jungle tribe," I responded.

Mart then asked me, "Have you heard the rest of the story?"

In October of 1999, I found myself with the now legendary Waodani tribe and Steve Saint, the son of pilot and slain missionary Nate Saint, who had originally launched Operation Auca. There I saw what Mart had called "the rest of the story."

I witnessed the incredible transformation of the Waodani people, as well as the miraculous power of forgiveness to change lives. Steve has represented the Waodani before the Ecuadorian government and speaks to countless organizations and churches worldwide about the ongoing struggles of the Waodani and their desire to reach others with the same message the missionaries brought to them.

Steve, along with his family, has lived with the tribe and has dedicated his life to assisting them in maintaining their culture in the midst of drastic, encroaching societal changes. For twenty-five years, the story of the martyred missionaries has remained dear and paramount to my life. I know that Steve and this message hold an important key to understanding missions in the twenty-first century.

Steve's writing, character, and message are poignant and unparalleled, continually reminding me of the importance of winning the lost at any cost. Prepare to be inspired, changed, and moved into action by this most powerful story. It is truly an honor to work in the kingdom alongside a man such as Steve Saint.

Tom Newman
President of Impact Productions
Tulsa, OK

The story of five missionaries speared in the jungles of Ecuador in 1956 has fascinated the world. Why did they go to such a dangerous place? What events led to their encounter with the Indians? How did the wives and families handle such a tragic loss? What has happened to them since that day? What about the Waodani tribe? What has happened to them?

Steve Saint, son of Nate Saint, the pilot, is one of the few who know the answers to these questions. His father was one of the five martyred along the river. He knows the feelings of those who first heard the news. He experienced growing up with his earthly father in Heaven. The love that was in his father for those tribal people got into him. Steve has given his life to reach these warriors with the Gospel of Jesus Christ. He forgave the ones who speared his father and loves them.

This epic is one of the most remarkable love stories in the history of the world. It is a continuation of the book of Acts. From the coliseum in Rome to the jungles of Ecuador, the sacrifice was the same. Love laid down its all for the King of kings. From lions to spears, people gave their lives to honor the One who took the nails.

Billy Joe Daugherty
Pastor, Victory Christian Center
Tulsa, OK

Steve Saint is a remarkable man! Through ministering to the people of Ecuador, his life serves as an awesome example of unconditional love. I am truly inspired by him.

Ron Luce
President and Founder
Teen Mania Ministries

Introduction

I get asked quite often to speak about "missions." I tell stories and make suggestions that I believe could help us do a better job. It is always exciting to have people tell me, as we shake hands afterward, that they understood what I was suggesting and would like to know more.

Well, this is "more." It is by no means intended to be a complete manual on missions, but rather a combination of ideas and true stories that will give you a little different perspective on Christ's Great Commission to us, His church.

My hope is that this book will spark your interest, your curiosity, and your excitement for what God has planned for you. The final curtain has not fallen. There are many parts yet to fill, and one of them has your name on it.

Chapter One

What man meant for evil, God meant for good.

On bare feet with widely splayed toes, six men moved silently through the dense green rain forest of the Amazon toward their objective. "Stone-age" warriors, they killed large game for their cooking pots with eight-foot spears—a crude but deadly weapon in experienced hands. They weren't after wild pigs or tapir; their quarry on this hunt was much more challenging and dangerous.

On a sandbar in the Ehuenguno river (labeled Curaray on maps), my father and four of his missionary friends were waiting excitedly for the arrival of these "savage" Amazon warriors. They had good reason to believe that they would come, and at least some basis to hope that the second meeting with this tribe, known to the outside world as "Aucas" or "naked savages," would be as friendly as the first one, two days before, had been.

The six Waodani or "true People" warriors were risking their lives. They watched the foreigners, spying on them from the shadows of the thick jungle underbrush, their naked bodies blending with their familiar surroundings. These foreigners had very light skin and covered their bodies with cloth. In the latter, they were like the Quechuas, the Waodani's historic enemies. Like the Quechuas, they also had "fire-sticks" with which to kill game and enemies at long distances. The warriors had only spears, a close range weapon.

For months, in attempt to fulfill a desire and obligation they had accepted from Christ as young men, my dad and his four buddies had searched for the elusive "Aucas." They knew they were there, but where? These jungle nomads moved from one small clearing to another, hidden by the towering jungle trees around their thatch roofed houses. They moved to follow game and to elude their enemies inside the tribe. Outsiders called them "Aucas," meaning "naked savages," because they wore no clothes and because they were killers.

> *Memories of atrocities perpetrated on the tribe by outsiders and complex intrigue within the tribe led the oldest and most seasoned killer to push for spearing these foreigners as they had so many others.*

The Waodani had accepted gifts dropped on a long line dangled from the foreigners' "wood bee" (plane) as it circled like a hawk above their houses, and they had returned gifts of their own. But memories of atrocities perpetrated on the tribe by outsiders and complex intrigue within the tribe led the oldest and most seasoned killer to push for spearing these foreigners as they had so many others.

All six warriors had killed people before, but never so many with so few. The guns these foreigners had, reduced their chances of success to the point of virtual suicide. Four of the six were somewhat reluctant participants but were caught in a tangle of circumstances too complicated for them to understand and too powerful for them to control.

The drama that these six naked Amazon warriors and the five young North American missionaries were about to participate in would shake their respective worlds, a fact that none of them had any way of knowing. What the five foreigners were attempting to do for God and for the Waodani would fail. But God would use their failure for a success greater than they could have ever imagined!

What the six warriors meant for evil, God meant for good. He had a role for both groups of young men in a story that He was about to write.

Forty-five years and several chapters later

Millions of Christians all over the world know the story of how Jim Elliot, Roger Youderian, Ed McCully, Pete Fleming and my dad, Nate, were speared by Waodani in 1956. Many Christians know part of the rest of the story, too, how after the five young missionaries were killed, God opened a door for Elisabeth Elliot and my aunt, Rachel Saint, to go live with the Waodani, and how when the Waodani heard the gospel of Jesus, many began to walk God's trail. The church has been inspired by the transforming and reconciling power of the gospel demonstrated when my sister and I were baptized by two of the men who had speared our dad to death. But for all the influence the Waodani story has had, and for all the missions effort it has inspired, the church has missed a crucial Great Commission lesson that the Waodani themselves have painfully learned: In a tragic irony, the sacrificial efforts of many believers on behalf of the Waodani almost

> *In a tragic irony, the sacrificial efforts of many believers on behalf of the Waodani almost destroyed the very church those dedicated believers labored to plant.*

destroyed the very church those dedicated believers labored to plant.

When the Waodani asked my family and me to come live with them after my aunt Rachel's death in 1994, I was dismayed to find that the Waodani church was less functional than it had been when I lived with them during school vacations while growing up. When I was a teenager, the Waodani had built their own churches. Now they let a church built for them by foreigners fall to disrepair, telling me they didn't know who it belonged to and so didn't have "permission" to fix it. When I was a teenager, the elders of the Waodani church baptized me; now the church had no identified elders, and they waited for outsiders to baptize their own people. I began to see what being "net receivers" had done to a proud people I had once known as "net givers."

The Waodani were feeling threatened by outsiders who were dominating more and more of their lives. They had grown increasingly dependent on outside medicines, trade goods, airplanes, schools, radio communications, and money. I was not surprised that the tribe felt threatened by oil companies, environmental groups, and the government. It was a major surprise to me, however, to find that they also felt threatened by all of the benevolence they were receiving from Christian missions and relief organizations.

It was a major surprise to me, however, to find that they also felt threatened by all of the benevolence they were receiving from Christian missions and relief organizations.

How could the efforts of believers have had such a different effect than they intended? Could help cause harm?

For nearly half a century, the Waodani had received the full benefit of twentieth-century missions strategy. Millions of Christians knew about them, many more than the typical number of Christians had "gone" to them, and much more money than usual had been spent on them. If current missions methods are effective, the Waodani should have been our star success

> *The twentieth-century model of missions leaves the vast majority of Christians out of the church's spiritual battle.*

story. Instead, after decades of missionary effort, while there was a group of individual Waodani believers, there was really no functioning Waodani church. How, in spite of our good intentions, had all this "help" almost destroyed the very church believers were commissioned to plant? As in so many other places where Christians work to fulfill the Great Commission, I believe the problem isn't a lack of sincere effort but a misunderstanding of the objective of the Great Commission and a resulting use of counterproductive methods. The twentieth-century model of missions leaves the vast majority of Christians out of the church's spiritual battle. The model could be summed up as, "Feed the world spiritual fish." That is an oversimplification, but as a generalization it isn't far from reality. Our commission on the other hand is more like, "Distribute spiritual fish samples and then train all those who want more to fish for themselves AND teach them to teach others to fish!" In other words, the purpose of missions is to plant indigenous churches that are self-propagating, self-governing, and self-supporting.

The twentieth century model has largely failed to do this and, consequently, it failed the Waodani. But consider

this: Even though thousands of incredibly talented people
are working to carry out Christ's Great Commission, and
even though more good things are happening now than at
any other time in history, billions of people haven't yet
heard Christ's gospel even once. Unlike the Waodani, many
of these vast numbers of peoples have never been heard of.
There are so many people, that even more missionaries and
more money under our current methods will never reach
them. Yet reaching them is our commission. To fulfill our
commission, we need a new paradigm; actually it is an old
one we need to go back to.

This is not the Great Option

Christ has commissioned us, His church, to distribute His offer of a free remedy against the fatal sin disease
that has infected everyone everywhere. The Christian
church has been working at this for twenty centuries. We
have done better in some of them than others. In the twentieth century we made a crucial mistake that debilitated
what was otherwise a great effort. We left most of the com-
batants out of the conflict. That great omission hurt us.

What is the solution? What can we do to strategi-
cally include the majority of troops we have left out of this
great spiritual struggle? First, there should no longer be
any question that the average Christian, here or there, who
supports ministry, teaches Sunday School, raises a godly
family, or uses his or her spiritual gift in offering service,
exhorting, leading, or showing mercy (Romans 12:6-8) is
critical to the spread of Christ's Gospel. We cannot hope to
fulfill our Great Commission unless we recognize our great
omission. Not all believers can or should be missionaries,
but every believer, regardless of his or her educational and

financial ability—or natural and spiritual gifting, has a place in missions.

Paul said this very thing quite succinctly in his letter to the believers in Rome. He told them, "Whoever will call upon the name of the Lord will be saved. How then shall they call upon Him in whom they have not believed? And how shall they believe in Him whom they have not heard? And how shall they hear without a preacher? And how shall they preach unless they are sent" (Romans 10:13-15a)? "Senders" are just as critical as "goers." Let's not make aces of the front line pilots without making heroes of the "Rosie Riveters" who are making their important role possible!

Second, it will not take hundreds or thousands more, but millions more Christians to turn the tide in this new century and get the Gospel message to the three billion people who still need to hear it. Does that sound impossible? It's not. Most of those

> *Let's not make aces of the front line pilots without making heroes of the "Rosie Riveters" who are making their important role possible!*

Christians are already in place, and they already speak the language and know the culture. Who are these people? They are the millions of indigenous believers all over the world. Most of them would need to be trained and equipped. Like the Waodani, many of them have been convinced that they aren't capable of helping win this spiritual conflict. In comparison to high-tech, highly educated missionaries, many of them feel quite "primitive." But then, in the jungles and slums and rural hinterlands of the world, a starched uniform and sophisticated technologies that break down in high humidity are not much good.

Whether we are believers working in our local church or missionaries laboring among an unreached people, whether we are indigenous to Europe or to the Amazon, our participation in the Great Commission has great consequence. The church's commission is quite specific. We are supposed to go into "all the world and preach the gospel to all creation. He who has believed... shall be saved, and he who has disbelieved shall be condemned" (Mark 16:15–16). That is an awesome responsibility with serious consequences if we fail. Ezekiel 33 suggests that we are the watchmen that have been entrusted to warn the people that the enemy is coming. If we warn people, two things can happen. Either they heed our warning and are saved, or they ignore the warning and die. But regardless of what they do, if we have warned them we are no longer responsible. But

> *I believe that Jesus gave us a formula for success along with His commission and that Jesus' disciples showed us how to put Jesus' plan into action.*

what if we don't warn them? The Bible simply says, "that wicked men shall die in his iniquity, but his blood I will require from your hand" (Ezekiel 33:8).

Warning everyone in the entire world that sin is going to kill them, and then explaining how to get the remedy, is a huge task. Half of the people living today haven't been warned. They speak thousands of different languages, many of them are hard to get to, and the majority of them live behind religious and political barriers that exacerbate the difficulty of delivering the diagnosis and the remedy. But that is our commission.

I am convinced that we can carry out this seemingly impossible task. I believe that Jesus gave us a formula for success along with His commission, and that Jesus' disciples showed us how to put Jesus' plan into action.

The Bible with a jungle twist

God had to take me to a lonely little clearing out in the Amazon jungle where I was trying to help in what I believed was a hopeless task before I was so desperate for answers that I actually began to see them. I had taken my family to live with the Waodani at their request. I love many of them. We are like family. I believed God had sent us to help them as He had sent my dad and his four friends. But lots of people more capable than I had been trying to help the Waodani for over thirty-five years. There was very little to show for all the efforts that had been expended on their behalf. I could not imagine what I could possibly do for the Waodani that all these other people and organizations were not equally willing and able to do for them.

I was OK while we were preoccupied with helping the Waodani build an airstrip, and while we were starting gardens, and building our little houses. I was OK while Ginny and our four children and I were still feeling the adventure of learning to live out in the rain forest with no roads, no stores, no electricity, no plumbing and no telephones. But when the novelty and the challenge of surviving had lost their bloom, I felt a substantial need to understand why

> *I could not imagine what I could possibly do for the Waodani that all these other people and organizations were not equally willing and able to do for them.*

God wanted me out in the middle of nowhere. I had spent years studying law and finance. I had invested a great deal of time and energy learning how to start and build businesses that were profitable. Now, I had taken my family out to the middle of nowhere to attempt an impossible task, just because I was sure that God wanted me to. Fortunately, my wife Ginny and our four children concurred.

> *I was sitting at a little table in our rustic jungle house reading the Bible by candlelight as bats dodged and maneuvered overhead when 1 Corinthians 3 suddenly made sense to me.*

I started searching for answers in scriptures that dealt with the purpose of missions. It is almost embarrassing to admit that something that now seems so obvious seemed like a revelation to me back then. In scriptures that I had been reading for years, I found the answers I needed. I was sitting at a little table in our rustic jungle house reading the Bible by candlelight as bats dodged and maneuvered overhead when 1 Corinthians 3 suddenly made sense to me. Paul told the few believers in Corinth that they were just babies, spiritually. They couldn't even handle solid spiritual food. They still needed milk. None of that was new to me. What was new was that it dawned on me that Paul was writing to these baby believers. He had gone off and left them to function as a church and to be productive members of Christ's family and they hadn't even been weaned yet.

Then in the old standard Great Commission verses in Matthew 28:18-20, I found another piece of the puzzle. Jesus said He had received all authority in Heaven and on earth to evangelize the world. Then, He did something unusual. After He said that He had the authority, He told His handful of followers that they should make disciples in all the nations. I knew that eleven common, ordinary, uneducated, and unprepared men (Acts 4:13) couldn't obey that command without supernatural backing and a good game plan. And then "I discovered America"; lots of people had been there before me, but I had never thought much about verse twenty. In verse eighteen Jesus said He had the authority to evangelize the world. In verse nineteen he told His disciples to do it for Him. And then in verse twenty

Evangelizing the world is like a relay race. In areas where there is no church, missionaries run the first lap. Then we should hand off to the local believers to finish the race.

He told them how to do it. Verse twenty is the piece I had been missing: the "how to." Jesus finished His commission by telling us to "teach" the people we reach "to observe all that He commanded" us to do!

Believe it or not, after being a Christian since I was a little boy; after growing up on the mission field; after being a missionary with experience in South America, the Caribbean, and Africa, these were novel ideas to me:

1. The purpose of missions is not to evangelize the world. Christ gave that commission to eleven simple but dedicated men who represented the church. The commission to the church is to evangelize the world. The purpose of missions is to plant the church where it doesn't exist so it can evangelize its world.

2. Missions is like scaffolding that is used to erect a building. It is just temporary to lend support until the structure can stand on its own. Then it is pulled away and moved to another location where it is needed.

3. Evangelizing the world is like a relay race. In areas where there is no church, missionaries run the first lap. Then we should hand off to the local believers to finish the race. Just like Paul, and just like us, they don't have to be superstars, just obedient; they don't make the seed and they don't make it grow, they just plant and water. Just like the Corinthians, if they can hold their own bottle, the Holy Spirit can take over from there.

A few more houses won't eradicate homelessness

"The cost of lumber for each house we want to build on our missions trip this summer has gone up from four hundred dollars to over six hundred dollars. We either have to dig deeper or build fewer houses for these poor people."

I was about to speak at a large and very missions minded church and one of the elders was giving the announcements. "We have to sell forty dozen tamales for each house now. First, go out and buy yourself a big freezer and then put your order in." He was kidding, of course—about the freezer anyway. I wish he was kidding about the tamales and the house-building mission as well.

Why? Because no matter how many tamales his church makes and sells, and no matter how many houses they build for poor people in Mexico, they are not going to accomplish their mission—unless their mission is to build a few houses in Mexico. If their purpose is to eradicate homelessness for poor people in Mexico, there is a much better way to do it. Their current efforts are a drop in the ocean of poverty and homelessness. If their objective is construction evangelism, I believe they are about to unwittingly do their cause more harm than good.

All the churches in North America cannot eradicate homelessness in Mexico, let alone the rest of the world. There just aren't enough Christians or enough money to allocate to it. We could probably blitz the border towns and make a pretty good showing. But as soon as the millions of poor people living further south heard about free housing on the border, a homeless migration would start. But, what if we would apply the equivalent of Matthew 28:20 to the need for affordable housing in Mexico. What if we would train and equip poor Mexicans to build their own houses? What if we would negotiate affordable materials and invent new techniques of construction to use materials such as adobes stabilized with a little cement to replace concrete blocks and wood. We could make home ownership an achievable goal for everyone in the great country of Mexico.

There are far too few Christian missionaries to evangelize the world. There are too few missionaries to even plant the church amongst every one of the thousands of people groups that have no witness. But if we will plant the church as quickly as possible where we can, and if we teach them to teach others how to teach others, then we can reach the world for Christ and fulfill our commission.

The Saint Family

Saint family with Waodani in front of their jungle home: (Saints, left to right) Steve (Babae), Ginny (Ongingcamo), Jaime Nate (Mincaye) and wife Jessica, Stephenie Rachel (Nemo), Shaun Felipe (Tonae) and wife Anne. (inset) Stephenie, who died in July 2000, with little Dawa. Both claim Mincaye as "grandfather." (second inset) Jesse Abram (Yeti) with wife Jenni Joy (sister of Jaime's wife Jessica).

Saints with Waodani at Rachel Saint's grave in front of Tonampade church building (building built "for Waodani" by generous "outsiders," proved not to be as great a blessing as givers intended). Dayuma in foreground to right of marker, fled from killings within the tribe. Living on the outside, she adopted Rachel as her sister and was then used by God to open the door for Rachel and Elizabeth Elliot to go live with her tribe. At Rachel's funeral, Kimo told the assembled people, "Teaching us to walk God's trail, Nemo came." These words are the epitaph inscribed on Rachel's grave marker.

Steve with sons Jaime and Shaun in West African country of Mali. They're inspecting low-tech but reliable means of transportation. Steve and his family were asked to establish a base for Mission Aviation Fellowship in West Africa during the terrible 1980's drought and resulting famine.

I-TEC Indigenous People's Technology & Education Center

The I-TEC research center and training facility is located at the Dunnellon Airport Commerce Center in Central Florida. This facility was made possible by gifts from several Christians who recognize the value of training and equipping indigenous believers to reach their own people.

I-TEC staff member Gene Walrath stands in front of plane built at I-TEC to evaluate possibility of making inexpensive aircraft for use by indigenous believers. This pre-fabricated plane can be carried on airlines as accompanied baggage and assembled on the field with simple tools.

I-TEC staff teach indigenous students skills needed to operate and maintain tools that can help them reach their own people for Christ. Here, two students learn how to weld at I-TEC's training facility.

I-TEC helps frontier believers enter the computer age. Computers are becoming essential for communication, translation, record keeping, and even teaching indigenous believers how to fly, which is demonstrated here in a simple computer-based flight simulator.

Steve with . . .

. . . Tementa and Mincaye at Amsterdam 2000, an international conference for itinerant evangelists from 209 countries around the world; the conference is sponsored by the Billy Graham Evangelistic Association. Mincaye gestures as he gives his testimony to approximately twelve thousand delegates.

. . . three of six Waodani warriors who killed his father Nate, Jim Elliot, Ed McCully, Roger Youderian, and Pete Fleming. From left to right, Dyuwi, Mincaye, (Steve), Kimo, and Dabo, who was part of same group but did not participate in killings.

. . . Aunt Rachel, showing her the remains of his dad's little Piper Family Cruiser, "5156 Henry," which were found by Waodani just before Rachel's death in 1994. The plane was washed from Palm Beach after Nate was killed in 1956.

. . . sister Kathy and two Waodani young people are baptized by two Waodani believers in front of the very beach where these two men, Kimo and Dyuwi, had speared Steve's father just a few years before. Mother, Marj Saint, and brother Phil watch from Palm Beach with Aunt Rachel and Waodani.

. . . old Miimo, mother of friend Tonae, after landing at her village. Upon hearing about God and becoming a God follower, Tonae, who was kidnapped as a little boy, returned to his own family group to teach them to "walk God's trail." They speared him, making him the first Waodani martyr. The tribe named Steve's son Shaun after Tonae.

I-TEC High-Tech Tools For Low-Tech Environments

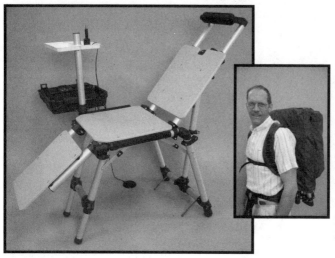

Developing an inexpensive but complete Portable Dental System powered by sun-light, which can be folded up and carried on an itinerant dentist's back, seemed like an impossible dream. The dream has become a reality, thanks to the creative help of I-TEC staff and volunteers. This unit can also be used as a medical examining table and a birthing chair. It weighs thirty-one pounds and includes a solar panel to recharge batteries for the I-TEC designed electric dental drill. It can be set up in three minutes and is small enough to be carried on an airline as accompanied baggage. Taking care of people's felt needs is a wonderful door opener for sharing the Gospel.

Designing dental equipment for use by indigenous people was only half the challenge. Training lay dentists is the other half. How do you teach someone to drill and fill teeth who doesn't read or write? How do you explain the causes of decay to people who have no concept of bacteria? I-TEC started with the realization that people who cannot read learn by observation. The answer was the development of a Non-Verbal Training Video series using video footage and 2-D animation. A significant side benefit of Non-Verbal Training is that, once perfected, it can be used in any field of study, by all language groups, without translation.

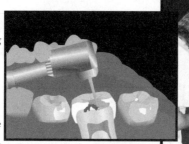

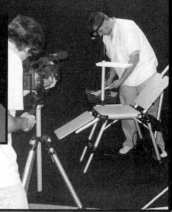

Powered parachutes are just one example of new technologies that can be adapted to enable indigenous Christians and missionaries alike to move from place to place where there are no roads. Transportation and communication are keys to efficiently spreading Christ's Gospel and fulfilling His Great Commission to us.

Waodani - Mission Vision Tours

Waodani women pose with Saint girls in front of traditional thatched "long house." Waodani built an authentic village in which to host Mission Vision Tours. The tours give outsiders an opportunity to see missions from the indigenous perspective while making a way for Waodani to financially support their ministry to their own people.

Two visitors are shown how to singe a monkey in preparation for the dinner pot. Living in another people's shoes helps sensitize visitors to those customs of ours that may seem strange to indigenous people.

Jungle rivers teem with interesting fish. The Waodani love to show visitors how to catch jungle fish like this one, which looks like a fresh-water barracuda.

Mission tour member gets a lesson in how to shoot a Waodani blowgun. This clever weapon is used to shoot birds and tree-dwelling animals such as monkeys for meat.

Hosting Mission Vision Tours has created an economy for Waodani believers, allowing them to support their own ministry for the first time. This is a common need shared by many emerging churches in frontier areas. The need to teach new congregations to be self-supporting is frequently overlooked in the process of church planting and inhibits new congregations from growing the churches that missions plant.

Appropriate Technology

Waodani powered parachute takes off from Nemompade on its maiden flight between Waodani villages in late 2000. A wild assortment of tubes with a parachute for a wing and a propeller-equipped jet-ski engine, this strange flying contraption is a dream come true for the Waodani. Designed for recreational flying, this unit has been modified by I-TEC staff and students, including Tim Paulson and Galo Ortiz, for use by the Waodani. Modifications include a cargo pod, new fuel system, and bush bars to protect pilot and passengers in case of a forced landing in jungle trees. Pilot Tementa can carry two passengers, cargo, or a stretcher patient. The powered parachute can carry over five hundred pounds, nearly twice its own empty weight.

Waodani field-test I-TEC "Gen-Cycle" as means of generating power without need for expensive generators that require scarce fuel and complex maintenance.

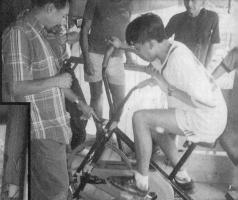

Young Waodani technician tapes testimony of another Waodani believer for their own radio program. Waodani were excited by this radio experiment, which was cut short by logistical difficulties in getting programs to capital city. From there, they were broadcast back to Waodani territory. The Waodani are praying for government permission to start their own radio station.

Technology In The Field

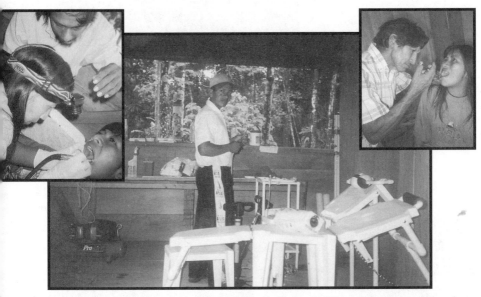

When the Waodani believers first began fixing their people's teeth, Dawa said, "Fixing their teeth, we will teach them to walk God's trail." Then she smiled mischievously and added, "And they can't even talk back." The Waodani Christians understand that the ultimate objective is not to fix hurting teeth but to cure the spiritual disease that is fatal to all people. Christians in a thousand tribes need this tool and tools like it to open doors so that they can share God's offer of salvation with their people.

Indigenous people everywhere want to learn how to use computers. With a laptop computer and a solar-powered printer and copier, two Waodani teenagers were able to translate and publish a short discipleship booklet. With these specialized tools, they were able to do in six hours what would normally have taken up to six months using standard methods. And they were able to do it themselves.

It is not enough for indigenous people to learn to use specialized technologies. They also need to learn to maintain them. I-TEC volunteer Steve Buer has found that some Waodani, just emerging from "the stone age," have natural mechanical ability. Without being able to speak their language, he taught Waodani men to overhaul an engine in one day. Giving "fish" is a temporary help. Teaching people to "fish" is a long term solution.

Aerial picture of a typical, modern Waodani village built around a rustic air strip. The Waodani live in approximately twenty-five small villages spread over six thousand square miles of rugged Amazon rain forests on the flanks of the Andes mountains in Ecuador, South America.

A picture of Nate Saint and "George," the only Waodani man he ever met on a friendly basis, has become a famous missions picture. Nenquihui, the man Nate and his four friends nicknamed "George," was fascinated by Nate's plane and finally got a ride by climbing in and refusing to get out. It is ironic that the elder the Waodani believers chose for Steve to train as their first pilot is Nenquihui's son, Tementa. Steve and Tementa have been digitally superimposed into the original picture, signifying the duty of each generation to train the next one to carry out Christ's desire that all people know His love for them.

Campus Crusade for Christ International founder and president, Dr. Bill Bright (who passed away in July 2003), and his wife, Vonette (co-founder), invited Mincaye, Tementa, and Steve to address the staff at their new international headquarters in Orlando. Mincaye shared his testimony after Tementa gave Dr. Bright a brief blowgun lesson. What a wonderful demonstration that people from different "worlds" united in Christ can work together to make God's offer of forgiveness known to all people everywhere. (left to right) Mincaye, Steve, Dr. Bright, Marj Saint VanDerPuy, Vonette Bright, and Tementa. (photo by Guy Gerrard)

Chapter Two

Is this mission impossible?

Our job is too big to finish . . . doing it our way!

Have you ever met a person who has enough enthusiasm for both of you? After a few minutes with him or her, you feel like you can climb the tallest mountain. "Why not?" the person asks. "I've done it myself!"

One such friend, an entrepreneur and businessman, was encouraging me to dream a little bigger and aim a little higher. We were talking about two unique pieces of equipment that would allow low-tech Christians around the world to offer medical services to their people and to evangelize and disciple them in the process. One piece, a solar-powered Portable Video Pack, could be used to show educational videos or evangelistic ones, like the *Jesus* film, and can draw a crowd anywhere there isn't electricity for conventional video equipment. The other, a self-contained, self-powered Portable Dental Operatory, doubles as a medical examining table and a birthing chair for problem baby deliveries.

How big of a market can there still be for God's offer after all the time and effort we have expended to publicize it for the last 2,000 years?

Trying to meet very real needs

My enthusiastic, aim-for-the-stars friend happens to have a lot of manufacturing and flying experience, so I respected his opinion. He started out making hang-gliders in his young and foolish days (he loved to fly cheap), but when he got tired of that—and of all the liability involved— he sold the company to pursue an interest in music. He quickly formed a band and got ready to hit the touring circuit.

The problem was that the only equipment he could find to hold the musical instruments and sound equipment was excessively heavy and took up too much room. Being an inventive fellow, he decided to design and build his own. It worked so well on tour that other groups asked him to build similar equipment for them.

In his garage he started making stands out of the same aluminum that he had used for building hang-gliders. Finally he decided to put his keyboard stand into full production. It took a lot of time and money, but he was banking on there being a big market for the stands he was mass-producing.

To his surprise, he couldn't build enough! "We were almost sold out the first month," he told me, "so we made another production run and sold out again in a very short time!"

"But what about Portable Dental Operatory units and Portable Video Packs," I asked him, "how many should we gear up to produce?"

He responded, "It's a big world out there!"
I was having a hard time visualizing a market as big as he was encouraging me to consider. To get the cost down to what I wanted it to be, so that believers in the very poorest

areas of the world could buy it, we needed to make a lot of portable operatories. How big is the market out there?

The numbers behind the marketing

How big is the market for what God is offering? Really, how big of a market can there still be for God's offer after all the time and effort we have expended to publicize it for the last two thousand years?

It is tempting to believe that all we have left to do is to mop up a few stragglers before the job will be done. But it is a big world out there. There are approximately six billion people in the world today. The figure is so large that the number of people it actually represents is difficult to imagine.

The Waodani also have a hard time with large numbers.

Tementa and Mincaye, two Waodani friends, were with me on a recent speaking tour around the U.S. and Canada when we visited the CN tower in Toronto. Our guide was telling us that it was the tallest freestanding structure in the world at over fourteen hundred feet just to the first observation platform. When he asked me to translate for Mincaye, I explained that in Tementa and Mincaye's culture, they don't use numbers very much.

The guide insisted that I explain, so I gave it a try. He had no way of knowing that the Waodani count one, two, two and one, two and two, and then they say "onompo omaempoquiae," which means as many fingers as there are on one hand. If there are more than five, eight for instance, they might say, "As many as the fingers on one hand, and two and one." Or they might simply put their hands together and say, "As many as on two hands" since eight is closer to ten than to five, and it is easier to clap your hands than to do the math needed to say eight.

From fingers, they go to toes. On our trip, Mincaye was regularly asked how many children he had. He would enthusiastically slap his hands together and then look down at his feet to add three more, but he was wearing shoes; he couldn't show his toes! Since ten is fairly close to thirteen, Mincaye just started telling people that he had ten children. He wasn't trying to mislead them; he just doesn't know how to re-tie his shoelaces.

Do we really comprehend how many people there are in the world right now who don't know who Jesus is or what God is offering them through His Son?

As the CN tower guide waited for me to tell my friends from the Amazon how impressive his building was, I figured it would be easier to illustrate the numbers to Mincaye and Tementa than to explain Waodani numbers to the guide. Fortunately, I didn't have to explain the word inch or foot because Mincaye's feet are short but very wide from walking jungle trails barefoot for almost seventy years. To get a shoe to fit him, we had to go to one that was about a foot long.

"If you put your shoes end to end," I tried to explain for the benefit of our zealous guide, "it would take this many shoes: tipaempoga go tipaenhua go tipaempoga go tipaenhua . . . [as many as my fingers and my toes and my fingers and my toes and my fingers]." The guide got the picture, but Mincaye—a natural PR man—didn't have a clue how high the tower was or even what a tower was. He did figure out that he was supposed to be impressed and acted the part perfectly.

It doesn't add up!

Most of us have a better handle on numbers than Mincaye does, at least until the numbers get really big. Do we really comprehend how many people there are in the world right now who don't know who Jesus is or what God is offering them through His Son? How could we? The actual numbers are mind boggling.

Of the six billion people living today, only about one in ten claims to be a Christian. Specific numbers are difficult to nail down, but as things stand now, only about half of the rest of the world's population has any real chance of hearing God's offer.

I should clarify that saving people is a role God clearly reserves for Himself. Jesus told His disciples that God is the one who does the choosing (Mark 13:20), and Paul said, "God chose us in Him before the foundation of the world" (Ephesians 1:4). Our role is to simply get the announcement of the offer to people and then to help those who accept the offer become productive at telling others (Matthew 28:18-20).

How big is the job that is left? Well, if you could adequately explain God's offer to one person every second, one day would be enough to reach a small city. One pay period would be enough to

> *People who are beyond the reach of roads are usually beyond the reach of electricity, commercial transportation, mass media, and the Gospel. The approximate number of people in this category?*
> *Eight hundred million!*

reach a major metropolitan area like Orlando or Dallas or the entire state of Montana. But at one person per second, it would take *100 years* to reach all the people living today who haven't heard that Jesus died to set them free!

And by the time the century was over and the three billion people heard the Gospel, the population would have already doubled!

If a people group is beyond the reach of roads, they are usually beyond the reach of electricity, commercial transportation, and mass media. There are approximately eight hundred million people like this who also have had no access to the Gospel. These are generally the most difficult people to get Christ's message to because they are usually hidden behind both a language and a geographical barrier.

If just these hidden people without access to the Scriptures were to line up heel to toe, they would stretch completely around the earth at the equator *twice*, with enough left over to make it around once more following the prime meridian through the poles. This seems impossible, but there would still be enough left to stretch from California all the way to Europe.

Or if you think more clearly with dollars and cents, imagine six billion dollars (one dollar for every person in the world) sitting in a Swiss bank account. If you were granted just the interest at 10% per year, you would be a millionaire in only fourteen hours!

The reality of crunching numbers

We know how many people need Jesus Christ, but can we reach them all with the number of missionaries we currently have? Right now there are approximately 100,000 missionaries in active service in the world. That is a lot of missionaries, but is that enough to get the job done?

When Jesus was on earth and the multitudes were following Him, He told His disciples, "The harvest truly is plentiful, but the laborers are few. Therefore pray the Lord of the harvest sends out laborers into His harvest" (Matthew 9:37-38). At that point, Jesus was training His twelve disciples and was addressing seventy more that He was sending out two at a time (Luke 10:1). That makes a total of eighty-two. By comparison, 100,000 is quite an army, but there are a lot more people in our world than there were back then.

If you really don't have a handle on whether there are enough missionaries to get the job done, you are not alone. Most Christians are confused about this, and those of us involved full-time in missions are largely to blame. We have a tendency to regularly point out that we need more people (and money and equipment and . . .), but at the same time we keep reporting to those who support our ministries just how successful we are being.

Yes, missionaries are partly to blame, but they do have an excuse. If they don't regularly report that more people and money and equipment are needed, individuals back home will assume that the job is getting done, and recruiting, giving, praying, and going will taper off. On the other hand, if missionaries don't emphasize all the success they are having, the individuals and churches that support them with new missionaries, money, prayer, and equipment will assume they aren't being very effective and will quite easily find another organization or missionary to support—one who *will* report success.

But reports of success can be misleading as well.

A friend of mine opened my eyes to the reality of this when he described what happens in the area where he works in Mexico. "Short-term mission trips from the U.S. have been coming here for years," he pointed out, "and the results

have been amazing! Entire neighborhoods have gone forward to accept Christ at evangelistic events."

There is obviously nothing wrong with that, but my
friend continued.

"One day I happened to be with several of the local
people when they had a special meeting to decide who would
go forward at the next foreign missionary's altar call. I
couldn't believe my ears! They wanted the gifts (often a bag
with pencils and Bible literature) *and* wanted the missionaries to come back again. I asked one of the leaders how many
times he had gone forward to receive Christ, and he said,
'About a dozen times.' Then he added, 'If we all go up, the
missionaries won't believe it. We have learned that half or
two-thirds is a good number to keep them coming back.'"

Despite the games played with unsuspecting foreign
missionaries, and in spite of great actual missionary
progress, the number of people truly needing to hear of
Jesus Christ is increasing due to population growth in areas
that are difficult to reach.

Getting a handle on the numbers

For years I've been trying to find creative, new ways
to compare the size of the task with the number of people
who have committed themselves to doing the work. Not
long ago and right before I was to leave for a speaking
engagement on missions, I awoke with an idea. I took two
long tapes, one to represent the size of the missionary task
and the other to represent the number of missionaries. I
wanted to show how many of the people who don't have the
Gospel could be reached by all existing missionaries using
current methods.

To relate them to each other, I needed to project how
many people each missionary could be expected to reach. If

the job was to hand out Bibles, each missionary could cover a lot of people, but the Great Commission is much more involved than just handing out Christian literature. Combine the concept of Christ's commission to His church, found in all four Gospels, and paraphrase it, and you would end up with something like this:

> *God, my Father, sent me* (John 20:21) *to represent His interests on earth and gave me His authority in Heaven as well as here on earth to get the job done* (Matthew 28:18). *With His authority, I am sending you* (Luke 10:3) *as my representatives. Every people group on earth should be told so that they fully understand about repentance for forgiveness of sins* (Luke 24:47). *So, go into the entire world and teach everyone everywhere. Those who believe and are baptized will be saved! Be sure to explain carefully that anyone who doesn't believe is going to be condemned* (Mark 16:16). *Then train those who have decided to follow me— men and women and girls and boys from all over the world. Teach them how to do it themselves* (Matthew 28:20).

Most Christians feel that the Great Commission is really a call to send pastors to foreign countries along with backup personnel to help in technical and administrative areas. A hardworking pastor can evangelize, disciple, and oversee about five hundred people with a small but efficient staff. The exact numbers we use are not terribly critical, but let's assume that each missionary evangelist or church planter can do the same. This is the multiplier that will allow us to measure the efforts of world missions against the job Christ has entrusted to us.

Next, I took the three-hundred-foot tape representing three billion (3,000,000,000) people and divided it into feet and inches. One inch represented 833,033 people, which means the length from the tip of your thumb to the first joint represents about one million people.

At the meeting the following night, I asked several volunteers to unwind the 300-foot roll of red surveyor's tape. By the time they ran out, red tape was running down every aisle and across the sanctuary several times. I kept

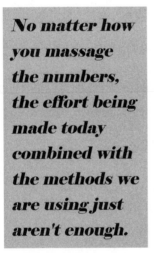

No matter how you massage the numbers, the effort being made today combined with the methods we are using just aren't enough.

looking at my thumb as the tape was being stretched back and forth, thinking of my daughter, Stephenie, who had died less than three months prior to this meeting. As I looked at that tape, I realized that God loves each of the three billion people represented by the red tape just as much as I loved my only daughter.

My grief was and still is overwhelming. Without the confident hope that God is now taking care of her and that because of Him I will get to spend eternity with her, I would be bitter, angry, and heart-broken. At that meeting I realized in a way that I never had before the agony that God must feel for all His children who are dying of sin. There was no human remedy that could have saved my daughter, but what if there had been? What if that remedy had been available, but the medical staff forgot to tell me or just did not want to be bothered? I can't bear to think about that, so how can I really understand how God must feel?

After rolling out the red tape to represent the task we have before us, the volunteers rolled out a blue tape to represent the people who could potentially be offered Christ's remedy *by all the missionaries combined.* One hundred thousand missionaries multiplied by five hundred prospective disciples each translated into sixty inches of tape.

Those sixty inches—five feet—of blue tape looked awfully short that night.

I doubt if the comparison affected anyone more than it did me. Numbers bore most people, but I know God isn't bored by these figures because they represent real live individuals. Each lost person is a son or daughter for whom God yearns.

At our memorial service and later by e-mail and letter, many people expressed how deeply sorry they were for our loss of our daughter. Many of them said, "I can't imagine how this must hurt." They are right; they can't know until it happens to them. Family and new grandchildren help comfort us, but they don't fill the hole left by Stephenie. Can you imagine our grief multiplied millions of times?

I am beginning to understand that no matter how many people hear God's offer, the hole in God's heart will remain, as long as there is even one child out there who could be saved and restored to Him if we would just tell them where to get the remedy.

Searching for solutions to the numbers game

There are thousands of talented and dedicated God followers working in many wonderful mission organizations who are attempting to complete our corporate task. Incredible new technologies are making their efforts more efficient than could have been dreamed of just a short while ago. But no matter how you massage the numbers, the effort being made today combined with the methods we are using just aren't enough. It truly is a "mission impossible."

One proposed solution is to give more money and send more missionaries. For this to work, consider how many more people would need to go and how much more money would have to be given to send them. Remember the red tape wrapped around the auditorium, representing what needs to be done? The tiny blue tape showing what is being done covered less than one arm-spread.

Giving more and sending more are parts of the solution but only parts. If you double the present number of missionaries *and* the finances, you could theoretically reach twice as many people—ten feet of blue tape. Now you only have 290 feet of red tape to go!

What other options exist?

I am convinced that the solution will require a paradigm shift back to the strategy that Christ taught and that the early church used very effectively. The solution is contained in the Great Commission. Jesus said to go into all the world, preach to all creation, make disciples of all nations, and baptize those who believe. But He did not say we had to do it all by ourselves! It is numerically impossible for missionaries to evangelize and disciple and pastor the entire world. Jesus concluded the Great Commission by saying, "Teach everyone to do just what I'm telling you to do" (Matthew 28:20, paraphrased).

In other words, we need to change our mindset to accommodate the fact that we cannot accomplish the Great Commission by ourselves. Every believer from every church, denomination, country, and race needs to play his or her vital role in the process. We cannot exclude anyone. There is a key role for every believer and a wonderful sense of significance that comes with it. We can't add everyone into the kingdom; we have to multiply them in.

This paradigm shift could radically affect everything missionaries and new believers do, say, and think. Yes, we have a big job to do, but together, with the Holy Spirit's help, we can accomplish it.

Summary—putting hope back into the numbers

We are indeed facing a seemingly astronomical number—three billion (3,000,000,000) people who have yet to receive the offer Jesus Christ made them. The numbers may be stacked against us, but there is hope in the same statistics.

We have approximately 100,000 missionaries to work with. If each of those missionaries were to evangelize and disciple and oversee five hundred people each, we would be able to cover fifty million (50,000,000) people. That is a lot of people, but it represents less than two percent of the three billion Christ wants us to reach.

What if we change the strategy and just ask each missionary to train sixty national believers in a given area? And what if we helped equip those sixty nationals to evangelize and disciple and pastor five hundred people each? Do the math:

100,000 missionaries x 60 indigenous trainees
x 500 given the Gospel by each trainee = 3,000,000,000 people!

Imagine reaching half of the world's population with the Good News of who God is and of His love for them and of His place waiting for them! It is still a huge task, but approached this way, we would be a lot more efficient in getting the job done!

An important ingredient in getting the job done is to encourage and make it possible for every believer to take part. It is especially critical to include indigenous believers in the plan because they know the language and the culture *and* because Christ told us to in the Great Commission. Not only is it the effective thing to do, but it is the obedient way to do it!

Reaching our world with the Gospel of Jesus Christ can happen, but it will take a shift in our thinking to accomplish it. Reverting back to the strategy that Jesus proposed makes it possible for the Mincayes of the world to be involved too. It is truly possible! Maybe we all need to aim a little higher and dream a little bigger.

Chapter Three

The deception of dependency

Good intentions can undermine
the church we are sent to plant!

I was amazed when we moved to Mali, West Africa, to find political and military influences from both the Soviet Union and the United States there.

One day I gave a coin and some food to a leper who was begging on a street corner and was immediately approached by several Maliens! I thought I must have offended them. Instead, they were very friendly. They told me they had been trying to figure out if I was American or Russian. "We couldn't be sure because there are so many of both in our country. When we saw you give money to the leper," they confided, "we knew you were American. Russians don't give anything without asking for something in return." (It is rare that anyone does. There are almost always strings attached.)

Back in the mid-eighties, Russians and North Americans didn't mix well. When I asked why there were both Russian and American functionaries in the same country, I was told by Maliens that both of those governments wanted to have influence in their country. They explained that the Malien government didn't want either one to leave. They had learned to play one against the other to maximize the foreign aid and military hardware they received. Mali could not survive without substantial gifts from outside the country. Some U.S. embassy employees explained it this way: "We pretend to help them, and they pretend to like us."

The cycle of dependency

Sadly, the same thing is happening in missions all over the world. The "haves" give to the "have-nots," often in the hope of gaining influence with them. Frequently, the result is dependency that debilitates the local church by encouraging a welfare mentality.

The purpose of missions is to plant indigenous churches that are self-propagating, self-governing, and self-supporting. What happens with frequent regularity is that instead of planting an indigenous church we end up transplanting our own church to a new setting where it doesn't fit. We support it, so we feel we must govern it to protect our investment. When people from that country see a church that we fund and control, they come to the conclusion that it is our church. If they work to attract people to our church, they expect to be paid for it. We pretend we have built the church for them, and they pretend that they appreciate what we have done. Frequently, the real result is resentment toward both the missionaries and their Gospel.

Dependency debilitates the local church by encouraging a welfare mentality.

There is a strange psychological phenomenon that takes place in this type of situation. It is the opposite of what I call the benevolent torturer syndrome. In this syndrome, a jailer might beat his prisoner three times a day. The prisoner finally accepts this punishment as his due. Then one day the jailer only beats him twice. Against all reason, the prisoner feels gratitude toward the jailer.

In the mission equivalent, which we might call the "missionary rogue" syndrome, a foreign mission moves into an area. The missionaries preach the Gospel, start a clinic, build a school, provide the teacher, sell medicines, set up a radio to tie the community to the outside world, and fly in needed products that are sold in the mission store. All of this is done for the benefit of the local people with the expectation that they will appreciate it and will be open to the Gospel as a result.

But what happens, when dependency develops, is often just the opposite. The people who were very independent realize that they cannot get along without the missionaries and resent being dependent. If the missionaries quit giving any goods or services that were being offered, the people, who have begun to see the service as their right, resent what is being taken from them.

> *Not only is dependency one of the Devil's most effective barriers to the spread of Christ's message of forgiveness, but once it is established, it is extremely difficult to break.*

The parallel goes even further. *Perceptive nationals are quick to figure out that competitive dependency is preferable to helpless dependency, so they frequently invite other missions to come work in their area.* Now they can play one mission against the other, just like their governments play foreign aid organizations against each other. And all too often it works.

Breaking the dependency mold

Not only is dependency one of the Devil's most frequently used barriers to stop the spread of Christ's message of forgiveness, but it is one of the longest lasting. Once established, it is extremely difficult to break.

When we went to live with the Waodani, they started out from scratch building a small new community that was centrally located. They built an airstrip. Then we started building our houses. And when that was done, they wanted to build a clinic and a school. But no one even mentioned building a church. They seemed to be content to hold services on the ground under one of the elevated houses. A building doesn't make a church, so I didn't think much of it until I started flying to other communities and realized that all of them had school buildings but only one had a church building.

> **The purpose of missions is to plant indigenous churches that are self-propagating, self-governing, and self-supporting. What happens with frequent regularity is that instead of planting an indigenous church we end up transplanting our own church to a new setting where it doesn't fit.**

When I asked the Waodani Christians why they weren't building "God's houses," they simply told me they didn't know how. This was odd because when I was a kid, these same people built their own church building. The next time I was in the community where we had buried my Aunt Rachel, I took a look at the one Waodani church building.

It was rustic but very nice by jungle standards. It was built on concrete posts, with a board floor and siding, covered by a tin roof. I noticed that the floor was rotten in one corner where frequent rains blew in through the chain link windows.

I asked several Waodani men why they didn't fix the floor. They seemed perplexed. When they finally gave me an answer, it was this: "God's house, who does it belong to? We don't know." *They weren't fixing the floor because they didn't have permission.* They had not built it, and they had not paid for it; so they reasonably concluded it wasn't theirs.

I began to understand why they had not been building church buildings in the other communities. When kind missionaries with good intentions decided to help the Waodani by building them a "nice" church building, the message the Waodani read into this gesture was that the church

> *Anyone of superior education, superior technology, and superior financial ability who is attempting to help people of inferior capability has to guard against creating dependency.*

buildings they knew how to build, with split bamboo floors and thatched roofs, were not acceptable. They concluded that only foreigners are able to build proper God's houses, so foreigners should build all of them. They expected that when outsiders figured the Waodani needed more God's houses, they would come build more.

Foreigners came back to build school buildings in all the communities, but they never came back to build more church buildings. *The natural and reasonable conclusion the Waodani came to was that school is more important than church.*

In the early days of our current North American society, school met in the church. The result was that

Christian values and Biblical principles permeated our culture. But the church that we have planted in Waodani territory has the church meeting in the school. The result there has been to relegate both Christian values and Biblical principle to the periphery of the younger Waodani generation. As a result, stealing, fornication, lying, laziness, and materialism have almost no influence to hold them back.

The thought doesn't count.

We must bravely and honestly face the fact that good intentions are not an excuse for poor execution. *When, in the name of Christ's commission, we do for indigenous believers what they can and should do for themselves, we undermine the very church that God has sent us to plant.* It is understandable that we make mistakes, but it is inexcusable that the mistake of creating dependency has become the rule and not the exception.

If you are surprised to find that it is possible to try to do good and end up doing harm, you have plenty of company. The subject of dependency is a painful subject. It is rarely put on the table for discussion and evaluation. Anyone of superior education, superior technology, and superior financial ability who is attempting to help people of inferior capability in those areas has to guard against creating dependency. To do this we should borrow the concept "above all else, do no harm" from the world of medicine. Don't create one problem in order to fix another.

When I went back to live with the Waodani in my mid-forties, their church was less functional than it had been in my mid-teens. I don't mean to insinuate that there wasn't a solid group of very faithful believers, but there is a difference between having a group of believers and having a functioning church.

The church of Christ is an organism that consists of believers working together under a structure and authority instituted by God to carry out certain functions that individuals cannot fulfill on their own. That is why God gives different spiritual gifts to individual Christians (Romans 12 and I Corinthians 12). He wants us to work together.

Paul pointed this out explicitly when he wrote, "There is one body, and one Spirit . . . one Lord, one faith, one baptism, one God and Father of all who is over all and through all and in all" (Ephesians 4: 4–6). But then he clarified that everyone is not given the same gifts, nor is everyone called to the same function. He stated that God "gave some as apostles, and some as prophets, and some as evangelists, and some as pastors and teachers" (v. 11).

Paul went on to say that these apostles, prophets, evangelists, pastors, and teachers given by God are not to carry out the function of the church. Instead, their function is "the equipping of the saints for the work of service, to the building up of the body of Christ" (v. 12). The objective is to make the average believer part of the army, not to find champions who will do the fighting for them.

The local body of Christ was not intended to be dependent on outside evangelism and outside government and outside money over the long haul. Paul made it clear that for the body to be whole, we need every joint and every part working together, which "causes the growth of the

Instead of a self-propagating, self-governing and self-supporting church amongst the Waodani, there was just a group of individual believers.

body for the building up *of itself* in love" (Ephesians 4:16 [emphasis added]).

The goal of equipping each local body of believers in this manner has not changed in 2,000 years.

Learning the proper chain of command

As a businessman, I learned how critical it is to know what your business is and how important it is to have a plan. But when God made it clear that my family and I should accept the Waodani believers' invitation to go live with them and work for them, He didn't make it clear what exactly it was that we were supposed to do. That made the assignment much more difficult. I began to understand how Abraham must have felt when God told him to leave his relatives and his father's house and his country but didn't tell Abraham where He was taking him.

> **When in the name of Christian missions we do for indigenous believers what they can do for themselves, we undermine the very church that God has sent us to plant.**

When we first arrived in the jungle, my sons and I lived on the ground under plastic tarps with the Woadani while they were finishing their new airstrip. We spent a couple of weeks building our houses and starting gardens. After that, I needed to know what they wanted me to help them with.

The Waodani don't have any chief or other form of social authority. If they had, I probably would have made a common mistake made by Christians in other countries—taking my instructions from a political authority rather than from a spiritual authority like we should.

As soon as the frame of our house was up and we had the tarp roof stretched over it and a few boards nailed down in one corner, I flew Ginny and Stephenie out to join Shaun, Jaime, Jesse, the Waodani, and me. The news that Ongingcamo (Ginny) and young Nemo (Stephenie Rachel was given Aunt Rachel's name) had arrived attracted a lot of Waodani from neighboring villages. We had a big meeting, and I told the Waodani that I needed them to tell me what they wanted me to help them with. They were simply content that we had come, but I was still working with a foreigner's mindset and wanted to know what the plan was so that we could get to work.

No one wanted to tell me what to do. Waodani don't naturally have bosses or leaders. Finally, it dawned on me that I wasn't in the jungle to just be a part of the Waodani family; I was there as part of God's family within the Waodani. The church elders were the proper authority to tell me what to do.

So I asked the people who the elders were, but no one responded. I thought I had used the wrong word for elder, so I looked up several verses in the Waodani New Testament that Aunt Rachel, Cathy Peek, and Rosi Jung had translated. The word I had used was correct, so I asked several of the oldest believers who the elders were. They responded with a shrug of the shoulders, saying, "Ininamai" (we don't know).

"How could they not know who the elders are after thirty-five years of church planting?" I asked myself.

As the answer became clear, I began to understand just how fatal dependency could be. Faithful missionaries have given years and years of valuable time to help the Waodani spiritually. Besides that, the graves of five young missionary men and my dear Aunt Rachel are testimony to an incredible effort that has been made to plant the Waodani church, and they didn't even know who their elders were. I at least knew who the elders had been. My sister Kathy and I had been baptized by Kimo and Dyuwi, which was the work of elders. They were sitting there, so I asked them, "You were elders when you took Tamaya and me into the water; are you still taking new God followers into the water?"

They answered, "The foreigners take the people into the water."

Cowodi (foreigners) were flying the planes for the Waodani, installing and fixing their community two-way radios, distributing medicines to them, taking care of their sick, building their schools, teaching their children to read and write, and paying for all of it. I realized that it was natural for those same generous people to occasionally hold Bible conferences for them and baptize them and teach them how to follow God's trail.

> **You can't know how helpless, hopeless, and useless it feels to have to depend on others to do what the Holy Spirit is motivating you to do, until you have experienced it yourself!**

And I also realized that it had become natural for the Waodani to let them.

The end result of years and years of hard work by many dedicated people had largely been nullified by one simple trick of the devil. Instead of a self-propagating, self-governing, and self-supporting church amongst the Waodani, there was just a group of individual believers. They thought that their proper place in God's plan was to let outsiders, who were able to do the technical things that they could not do, perform the spiritual tasks that they could do. But that is not God's plan!

Not only does dependency hurt the people who become dependent, but it puts a huge load on the people they depend on. Dependency debilitates both the receiver and the sender. Another insidious characteristic of dependency is that it develops much easier and faster than it can be cured. In this aspect of missions, an ounce of Biblical prevention is worth a ton of painful cure!

Searching for solutions

What is the solution to dependency? There really is no single solution. I have witnessed many different instances of dependency. Finding one solution that fixes all the problems is not realistic. But whatever the solution, the overall goal must be the same: to establish churches that are self-supporting, self-governing, and self-propagating.

Not long ago a member of a missions committee called me and asked for my opinion. Her church had just finished constructing a pre-built church in Romania. The church building had been designed in the U.S., built in panels in the U.S., paid for by people in this church in the U.S., and shipped in containers to Romania, where it was erected by a work team from the U.S. As the keys to the church were given to the Romanian pastor at the dedication ceremony, she admitted, "I had a feeling that something just wasn't right."

She asked me what I thought was wrong with the scenario she had just described. But I think she had already figured it out for herself. There are many congregations in Romania without facilities to meet in. Many of those congregations are slowly and painfully building their own facilities with their own labor and with whatever materials they can buy or scavenge. Imagine what those other congregations, painfully working and giving to have a place to worship and teach others, felt when they found out that another congregation just like theirs found a church in America that would just give them a facility. My guess is that this generous church here in the U.S., in the process of building one facility, stopped the construction of many more. It is very possible that they planted a seed of dependency in people they will never even meet.

She concluded by telling me that she hoped they would never repeat what they had done. Next time they would consider not only the needs of those they help *but also the possible negative ramifications of the help they wanted to give.*

When we are honest enough to ask ourselves the hard questions, we stand a much better chance of finding the solutions we so desperately need. In helping others, as in so many other aspects of life, the hard choice is quite often the right choice.

Seeing Waodani dependency first-hand and feeling the pain it causes reminded me of a white author who wrote about discrimination against blacks in the United States. Refusing an interview, one man told the writer, "You'll never understand what it's like to be black until you are black like me." The author accepted the man's challenge and took medication that made his skin very dark. In that new condition he revisited the places and experiences that had formed his opinions. His book

> **Dependency debilitates both the receiver and the sender.**

revealed an important principle: Life really does look different from the other side of the fence!

Very few missionaries will have the unique opportunity of living with an indigenous culture in the same unique way that God has allowed me to. It is almost impossible to feel another man's pain until you have stood in his place. I don't think you can know how helpless, hopeless, and useless it feels to have to depend on others to do what the Holy Spirit is motivating you to do, until you have experienced it yourself!

Dependency versus interdependency

It is important to note that dependency and interdependency are very different things. Dependency is dangerous and potentially fatal to an indigenous church, but interdependency is natural and usually healthy.

When the Waodani told me they wanted to have a clinic of their own and wanted equipment to do their own dental work and their own plane to fly patients and medicines from place to place as they saw fit, I

> *It is unfortunate that outsiders want to give the Waodani what the Waodani ought to be paying for.*

was both elated and scared. I was excited that they wanted to take responsibility for their own people's needs, but helping them do it seemed like an overwhelming task. Unfortunately, friends back in the States offered to help by paying for the things the Waodani needed. I say "unfortunately" because I knew that the Waodani needed to pay for these things themselves, but the offer to have outsiders pay was extremely tempting.

I tried to convince myself that designing all the necessary equipment was a big enough undertaking. Learning to use that equipment and then teaching the Waodani to do it too added another huge challenge. Developing an economy for them so that they could pay for all of it was too big to even contemplate. But then I began to think through the process. If the Waodani couldn't buy the equipment, they couldn't afford to maintain it. And if they couldn't buy it or maintain it, then equipment wouldn't last very long. When they needed replacement equipment and when other tribes saw what the Waodani had and wanted some of their own, would our benefactors give to everyone else what they had given us?

When we are honest enough to ask ourselves the hard questions, we stand a much better chance of finding the solutions we so desperately need.

The significance of buying what you need *for yourself* is not only important and healthy for the indigenous church, but it is a principle that has been around for years. When thousands of men were dying of a plague because David had disobeyed God, he was desperate for relief. God told a prophet to tell David to offer sacrifices on a certain piece of land. The owner offered to *give* David the land and the oxen and the wood for the sacrifice, but David refused. He said, "I will not offer burnt offerings to the Lord my God which cost me nothing" (II Samuel 24:24).

In the church, God's gift is free, but paying a price to carry out His purpose for the church develops perseverance in the membership and gives longevity as a result. We must not steal this privilege from our indigenous brothers and sisters.

When I told the Waodani that the things they wanted would cost lots of *tucudi* (money), they weren't phased. "You showing us what to do, we will work very hard and get lots of tucudi," they assured me.

So we started doing Mission Vision Tours. We didn't have much of anything valuable to sell, but we lived in an exotic world of luscious flora and fauna that intrigue many people. We decided to invite outsiders to visit the land of "true people." I explained to the Waodani that they could guide the people, build a village for them to live in, and show them how to hunt with blowguns, make fire with sticks, and sleep in hammocks. The tours have been a great success. We can't take many tours each year because the logistics of getting people that deep into the jungle—and back out again—are substantial. But everyone involved, including the Waodani for whom it means lots of work, loves it. They work very hard and are wonderful hosts. The money they have made isn't much by our standards, but it is a fortune by theirs. They have made enough to pay for their dental equipment, solar panels for electricity, two-way radio, little clinic, pharmacy, store, and their own unusual aircraft.

A missionary friend of mine who was willing to be frank confronted me, saying that I had just traded one kind of dependency for another. He said, "They depend on you to help organize the tours, and they depend on the visitors to give them money." But is that the same thing? No, it isn't, *not by a long shot!* Dependency is getting something for nothing and growing dependent on it. Giving someone something they want or need in exchange for something you want or need is interdependence. There is a huge difference between the two. Dependency requires that some people be "net givers" in order that others can be "net receivers."

What happens when I buy a camera at Wal-Mart? Minolta needs Wal-Mart to sell their camera, Wal-Mart needs me to buy it, and I need Wal-Mart to have it when I need it. We are all interdependent, but none of the parties are "net givers" or "net receivers." If Wal-Mart won't sell Minolta cameras, K-Mart will, but if neither have them, I can simply buy another brand. I'll eventually get what I want because I have what the store wants—money.

Are the Waodani dependent on Mission Vision Tours? Yes, in the same way that the people on the tour groups are dependent on the Waodani to show them the Amazon. There are no "net givers" and no "net receivers." This is a healthy interdependency that has not only created an economy for the Waodani, but it has given many visitors the unique opportunity to live for a few days in an exotically different world and to see their own world from "the other side." The experience gives them a new perspective on life and allows them to see missions from the receiver's side. For the Waodani, leading these tours has finally given them an opportunity to show people the enchanting world in which they are the experts.

Summary: Dependency worsens with age.

Dependency is not just a welfare condition. It becomes an insidious state of mind that can debilitate generation after generation once it gains a foothold. In fledgling new churches, it can be a debilitating and even fatal disease.

The purpose of missions is to plant Christ's church with a local flavor amongst indigenous people groups. *The purpose is not to transplant our flavor of Christ's church for indigenous people to get used to.* Truly indigenous churches are self-propagating, self-governing, and self-supporting. The church is not truly indigenous until it can function on its own to carry out Christ's commission, without outside input. But the objective of developing independent churches is not so they will be independent. The reason for making churches capable of being autonomous is that every church has a mission to carry out. Political barriers come and go in foreign countries. When they come, outsiders frequently have to leave. If the church is dependent on outsiders who have to leave, the church can no longer fulfill its mission.

Another reason that all local churches should be capable of independently functioning is that this is the most efficient way to carry out Christ's Great Commission to His church. And this is the way Christ taught us to build His church. The objective in making churches independent from the missions that plant them is not to get rid of the missionaries.

> *The church is not truly indigenous until it can function on its own to carry out Christ's commission, without outside input.*

It is for national believers to take over the responsibilities of the founding missionaries so that the missionaries can move to another place where they are more desperately needed. There are still thousands of people groups that have no witness to tell them what Christ has done to save them. Freeing a missionary to move on also frees the local believers to do what God has commissioned them to do. What's more, the sooner an indigenous church can function on its own, the sooner it is likely to be able to send out missionaries of its own to help reach those other people groups.

Dependency has two very dangerous characteristics. First, it can be spread with good intentions as well as with malice; it is just as deadly a poison if given by mistake. Second, it is much more difficult to stop than it is to start; the best remedy for dependency is prevention.

Giving believers in a new church the means to support their church and the skills to govern it are just as critical as teaching them to share their faith. Becoming self-propagating is natural for most new congregations. Anyone can tell someone else how his or her life has been changed, and it is natural for a new believer to want to tell others what has happened.

Learning to be self-governing is more difficult, and learning to be financially self-supporting is frequently the most difficult of all. We do missionaries a great disservice when we measure their effectiveness primarily by the number of people in the churches they plant. The most spiritual thing they can do for a self-propagating church that can also govern itself is to help the people find jobs so that they can support the ministry. There is a bigger need in many areas today for missionaries with business skills than with advanced theological degrees.

It is a lot easier to give someone something than it is to teach them to make it, just as it is easier to give people a fish than it is to teach them to fish. If you give a man a fish, you have fed him for a day and probably created the beginnings of dependency. If you feed him for many days and then quit, he will resent you for it. But, if you teach him to fish, you have fed him for a lifetime and given him the ability to feed others.

Chapter Four

They do have what it takes!

Bank balances and degrees hung on a wall are not the primary qualifications for serving God!

I had just flown out of the jungles and was in a hurry to buy supplies, pick up mail, and run errands for my Waodani friends. I needed to be off the ground and headed back before 5:30 p.m. because there are no lights on jungle airstrips and no navigational aids. I didn't have time to chat when a missionary friend caught me to ask a favor. "We have a dentist visiting from South Carolina," he explained, "who came down to do dental work for missionaries. He would really like to do some work in the jungles, and I thought maybe you would take him in to Nemompade so that he could help out some of the Waodani."

His request seemed innocent enough, but he had no idea what the Waodani had recently been through. Would bringing in another dentist add to their current hurt and frustration, or would it provide the catalyst to bring both physical and spiritual relief to hurting people in outlying villages and possibly even other frontier areas around the world? Either way, I would have to decide quickly.

Free dentistry—what could be wrong with that?

If the question had been, "Will you take him into Nemompade so that he can fill a few teeth?" my answer would have been an immediate no. A few months prior, a missionary had arranged for another dentist to fly into a Waodani community just a few hours walk—or a couple minutes by air—from where we were living. On my way back home from delivering malaria medicines to another Waodani village, I dropped in to see how this dentist was faring.

It was quite an operation. The missionary and dentist and several assistants had set up shop in one of the tin-roofed school cabins. Outside they had a gas-driven compressor to power the dental drill and suction. There was a small generator to provide power for mixing the amalgam filling material and to provide lighting for the operation. There were gas cans and oil containers strewn about with air hoses and extension cords running from the various generators and the compressor into the one-room school building where the dentist was busily trying to give a Waodani teenager some hope of keeping his teeth beyond his early twenties.

"Time is money" means little to people who aren't governed by time or money.

Sweat was running down the dentist's face, and it was clear to me that he had been hard at it since arriving the day before.

The Waodani from that village were all gathered around, waiting their turn, and Waodani from other villages were beginning to arrive by trail. It had been a long time since a dentist had visited this part of the jungle to fix rather than pull teeth, and since almost everyone has bad teeth, almost every Waodani in the area was waiting in line. The engines played a cacophonous duet as their respective governors tried to maintain a steady RPM under constantly varying loads. The compressor chugged and periodically wheezed, reaching its pressure limit, as the two-cycle generator emitted a generous cloud of smoke from what appeared to be an excessively rich mixture of oil in its gasoline. I was impressed, not only by all it took to fix teeth in the jungle, but also by the commitment of a Christian dentist who took a vacation from his practice to travel all the way to the Amazon jungle with his family to do the very thing he was taking a vacation from.

> **"Why do the foreigners fix just a few people's teeth? All these other people, their teeth hurting, what about them?" Dawa asked. What could I say to convince her that the doctor had other more "important" things to do?**

After draining some fuel from my plane to augment their dwindling supply, I took off for home. Later that afternoon I heard two planes land and take off at the village where the dentist and his team were working. I asked our Waodani neighbors what was going on, and they nonchalantly answered that the foreigners were probably just leaving. I didn't believe that they would be leaving so soon after spending so much time and effort getting set up, and there was no way they could have taken care of even a fraction of all the Waodani waiting and desperately needing to have their teeth fixed.

I was tired, but a couple Waodani men offered to help fuel the plane and suggested we go see what had happened. When we landed, it was clear that they were right. Every trace of the dental operation was gone, except for the crowd that had been waiting their turn. I asked why the *doctodo* (doctor) had left. "Ononki," they responded, which means for no reason, they just left.

Why does the doctodo fix only a few teeth?

"Well, at least they fixed some teeth, and something is better than nothing," I thought to myself. The Waodani, however, did not see it that way. My tribal grandmother, Dawa, came up to me and asked the question that was on all of their minds: "Why do the foreigners fix just a few people's teeth? All these other people, their teeth hurting, what about them?"

I tried to explain that the *doctodo* had come from a long way away and that he had many foreigners who were also waiting to get their teeth fixed. I did not bother trying to explain that "time is money" in the outside world and that it cost him lots of *tucudi* to come and even more to stay. Dawa and the older people who dared state the obvious told me that they did not see what had just taken place "well." They added, "We say a doctodo, living here, should come to help us all the time."

> *The Waodani wanted a full-time dentist to live in the village, but the support alone, for such a missionary dentist, would be greater than the entire Waodani gross national product.*

I could literally feel the frustration and sense of helplessness that everyone around me was feeling, but I knew having a resident dentist would never happen. Nor would it be justifiable for a full-time dentist, whose support would be greater than the entire Waodani gross national product, to come live with them. I was the only one present who understood how foreigners think, so the people were waiting for my response.

"The foreigners will never send a doctodo to live here. If you want to have your teeth fixed all the time, one of you will have to learn to do it," I blurted out without thinking over the ramifications of what I was saying.

Dawa shot back just as quickly, "You teaching us how to do it, we will do it ourselves!"

The discussion continued for some time, and I realized that the Waodani were serious about not wanting to have foreigners come in to do things for only a few when it meant leaving the rest of them feeling worse off than they had been.

The old saying "everything is relative" applies here. From the Waodani perspective, those with bad teeth who had walked the trail with the hope of having them fixed were better off *before* there was hope than after it had been removed. For one thing, before the dentist came, they were all in the same boat. No individual had fixed teeth. Now those who still hurt had to face the fact that they had almost found relief, and on top of that, they had the few who had found relief to remind them of how unfortunate they were.

In the Waodani culture, there was no class distinction. Everyone lived in a thatched hut, wore only a G-string for clothing, grew the same food in their gardens, hunted the same game, and shared whatever they had in excess. There was no way to build a net worth, no reason to build a bigger house than necessary or to make more hammocks or pots than needed. There was no competition for climbing the social ladder because there was no such ladder to climb. Contact with the outside world introduced the perception of need for things, such as dental services, that they never knew existed. When the benefits of those services became known, a perceived need developed, along with a tension to acquire those services.

And when some people receive benefits and others don't, that tension is increased substantially. It is a tension that the Waodani don't know how to deal with. I watched the effects of this social tension grow after the departure of the missionary dentist. I thought the people should have been grateful on the whole for what these outsiders had done for them.

> **A perceived need is an incredible force among indigenous people.**

But I was also beginning to understand their frustration and sense of helplessness at not being able to control what was done for them or how it was done or when it was offered.

For lack of anything to say, I asked them, "What do you see well?"

Dawa spoke for the group with several others affirming their agreement: "We think no foreigners should come to fix some people unless they fix all the people."

Bad teeth are a major source of suffering and a gateway for many infections that cause additional sickness and suffering among the Waodani. They needed a dentist but were deciding on the spot that they didn't want any more dental excursions into their community. They then told me again that they wanted me to teach them how to do what this dentist had shown them could be done to relieve their suffering. There was one glaring problem—I didn't know how to fix teeth, and I assumed it would take years for me to learn and then more years to teach them.

I negotiated for an alternative, "Would you see it well if the foreigners sent a doctodo to teach you how to fix teeth?"

Dawa's response was immediate. She inhaled audibly, signifying assent, and then said, "Tell them to come teach us!"

Could the Waodani become dentists?

When I was suddenly faced with the possibility of bringing in the dentist from South Carolina, I thought to myself, "Well, here's my chance. This is an opportunity to give the Waodani some dental training." So I said the dentist could come on one condition: that he be willing to teach the Waodani what he was doing.

I also had a private reason for considering this little experiment. I had already brought my family out to Shell Mera for a couple days of speaking English, eating fresh vegetables and ice cream, and enjoying a little privacy, which is almost non-existent in Nemompade. I figured that no dentist could teach anyone much in one day, which was all the time that this dentist and his pastor, who was working as his dental assistant, had to offer. But I had also been looking for an opportunity to show the Waodani that they could host people from the outside on their own, without needing me as a go-between. If this dentist and pastor couldn't teach the Waodani how to fix teeth in one day, at least

Not being able to control what is done for you, or how or when it is done, can breed frustration and helplessness!

their visit would make an interesting experiment in unchaperoned, cross-cultural exchange. It would be quite an experience, since the dentist and his pastor had never been in the jungle before and couldn't speak any language the Waodani understood.

The dentist had borrowed some of the same semi-portable dental equipment that I had seen in operation just a few weeks before. I loaded the two *cowodi* (foreigners) and equipment until my little bush plane was bursting at the seams, and we were off. When we arrived, everyone in Nemompade came to our house to meet the visitors. (I assume that was their reason, but I can't be sure. It seemed like everyone in the village was over at our house every night unless we went to one of their houses. The Waodani live to live, and any event is sufficient excuse to have a party.)

Early the next morning, all the Waodani were back to see what the foreigners were going to do. I explained to the two soon-to-be-very-alone outsiders that I had to start making flights that the Waodani elders had previously asked me to make, and I assured them that they would be in good hands and that I would be back late that afternoon to check on them. They were a little nervous about being alone without the ability to talk to anyone, but the Waodani were being charming and friendly. As I walked to the plane, my conscience was telling me that I couldn't leave these two visitors and the people alone when they were about to embark on such an important experiment.

I also knew the two outsiders couldn't set up by themselves because they needed our generator and the little air compressor that the Waodani would have to find and get operating. I was dying to pretend I had left and then sneak back to watch what was about to happen, but I couldn't. Everyone would be waiting to hear me take off.

When I came back late that afternoon, I found the two dentists in our house surrounded by Waodani, obviously at ease and having a good time. I was anxious to know how things had gone with both the dental and the cross-cultural experiments. Before I could ask, the dentist had a question of his own.

"Steve, you told me that nobody here knows how to repair teeth."

"They don't," I responded, not sure what he was getting at.

"Yes, they do," he responded confidently.

"No, they don't," I replied, thinking that maybe he was just building up to telling me that he had taught someone to do some minor procedure.

"Yes, they do," he repeated.

At that point I lost my patience. I was tired and hot and dirty and coming down off the adrenaline rush that is a regular part of flying in and out of short, rugged jungle airstrips in a little plane that wasn't really designed for that.

"I have known these people all my life," I replied a little more directly than necessary, "and no one has ever taught them to do anything with teeth but pull them! You have been here less than twenty-four hours and . . ."

He cut in and said, "I spent five years in dental school and have practiced dentistry for over fifteen years. I'm telling you that someone here knows how to prep teeth [prepare teeth for filling]." He went on to explain that it had been hot working out on the riverbank. They had set up there in the bright sun because we had no other source of light adequate to work by. "I gave that young lady anesthetic," he said, pointing to one of the teenagers, "and then came up to the house to rest and to get something to drink while it was taking affect. When I went back, her teeth were already prepped and ready to fill. I don't know who did it, but whoever it was knew what they were doing."

I didn't know what to say, so I asked the Waodani who had fixed Mangade's teeth. No one admitted to it, but Tementa, an old friend who is recognized as one of the Christian elders, had a funny look on his face. Several people glanced at him when I asked who had used the drill to fix Mangade's teeth. Sure enough, it turned out to be Tementa!

Tementa said a little sheepishly, "I saw that the doctodo had already given her the thorn [shot], so I thought 'What could I hurt?' And I did it."

When the dentist heard that Tementa had had no dental training at all, he was amazed. "In dental school after sixteen years of previous formal education, we were well into our second year before they would even think of letting us drill a patient's teeth. If the Waodani can do what he did today with no training besides just watching me for a few hours, they shouldn't be pulling teeth; they should be fixing them!"

I agreed with him, but neither of us knew where to go from there. Finally, we decided that I would fly to the dentist's hometown of Orangeburg, South Carolina, the next time I was in the U.S., and he would give me some training that I could pass on to the Waodani. What we hadn't considered was how to find affordable equipment that was appropriate for an Amazon setting where there was no electricity, no gas stations, and no dental supply houses for replacement parts.

> "If the people can do what he did today with no training, other than just watching me for a few hours, they shouldn't be pulling teeth; they should be fixing them!"

Never underestimate another person's ability.

It is amazingly easy to make the dangerous assumption that people without formal education lack intelligence and capability.

Apparently, this was common in Jesus' day as well. Peter and John were going to the temple to pray when a cripple who had to beg for a living asked for some money. They didn't have money, but Peter, realizing that the same name by which they prayed to God had power to heal physical as well as spiritual problems, told the poor fellow, "In the name of Jesus Christ the Nazarene—walk!" (Acts 3:6) They probably knew as well that by demonstrating concern and power over physical ailments they could convince people to trust God through Jesus for their spiritual ailments. Peter believed that God would heal the man and grabbed the cripple by the hand and pulled him to his feet. When he let go, the cripple was healed! By God's special intervention, he could walk on physical legs, but as a result of Peter and John showing interest in his physical needs, five thousand men (in addition to who knows how many women and children) began to walk "God's trail," as the Waodani would put it.

The next time I was in the U.S., I flew up to Orangeburg long enough to get two days of dental training and to pick up some used equipment to modify for use in the jungle. Then I went back to teach two Waodani volunteers, approved by the elders, what I had learned. I was concerned that they would see this as an end in itself. I was hoping that—like the healing of the

> *It is amazingly easy to make the dangerous assumption that people without formal education lack intelligence and ability.*

cripple—it would just be a means to the Waodani's teaching other Waodani in other villages how God could heal the rot in their hearts that didn't throb like their abscessed teeth but that was much more deadly.

I didn't need to worry. As soon as I delivered the equipment and started teaching Nemonta (Tementa's wife) and Gaba (the son of an old friend who became the first Christian martyr amongst the Waodani), Dawa informed me publicly, "Fixing people's teeth, we will teach them how to walk God's trail."

When Annas and the other political and spiritual honchos called Peter and John in to put them in their place, they knew that Peter and John "were uneducated and untrained" (Acts 4:13). They too had mistakenly assumed that uneducated was the same as ignorant. They couldn't figure out why Peter and John were so confident, let alone how they could have healed a badly crippled beggar.

Then it dawned on them that that qualifications these simple men had for effective preaching, boldness before earthly authorities, and ability to pray down power to heal people did not come from a classroom experience and wasn't dependent on a degree that could be hung on a wall. Peter and John were seen as having what it takes because they "had been with Jesus" (Acts 4:13). And they wouldn't be intimidated into keeping quiet. They said to the religious leaders, "Whether it is right in the sight of God to give heed to you rather than to God, you be the judge: for we cannot stop speaking what we have seen and heard" (Acts 4:19-20).

Dawa, an illiterate (she can't read letters on a piece of paper and understand what they mean, but she can read the weather and the trail of an animal in the jungle), stone-age, old grandmother, shares with Peter and John a lack of formal education and training. But she and her husband, Kimo, serve under the same commission that compels you and me to "go into all the world and preach the Gospel to all creation" (Mark 16:15), "making disciples of all nations" (Matthew 28:19). They also share access to the same power that Peter and John called on to heal the lame man. The promise in Acts 1:8—"You shall receive power when the Holy Spirit has come upon you; and you shall be my witnesses . . . even to the remotest parts of the earth"—refers to Waodani God followers as much as it does to any of the rest of us.

Dawa and Kimo were the first two Waodani living in their native culture to accept God's offer and to start walking His trail. They didn't hear about God from a missionary. God used a young girl named Dayuma who had run away from killings within the tribe to tell them the few Bible stories that she had heard from my Aunt Rachel while Aunt Rachel was trying to get Dayuma to teach her the Waodani language. When Dayuma had told the little she knew about creation and how God had sent his Son to die so that the people could live, Dawa and Kimo were thrilled. They bombarded her with questions, most of which she couldn't answer. Dayuma said that she would bring Aunt Rachel, the foreigner whom she had adopted to replace Nemo (star)—a sister who had died—and another foreigner whom she called Guikade (meaning woodpecker—Betty Elliot) to teach them more.

Dawa and Kimo would not agree to wait. They were afraid that Dayuma might be bitten by a poisonous snake or killed by evil spirits in the form of a jaguar. "Teach us again everything that you know about God," Dawa and Kimo insisted. "Then if you don't come back, we ourselves will teach the people."

Dawa and Kimo are still uneducated and untrained in most people's opinion, but they are true God followers and have had a powerful influence in the lives of both non-believers and believers, including myself. When I was a teenager, Kimo and another Waodani man baptized me along with my sister and two Waodani youth. Kimo also helped kill my father when I was a little boy. Through that event, God used Kimo to help shake up a Western Christian world that had grown apathetic to His commission.

In 1966, Kimo and Come (Dayuma's husband) spoke to thousands of delegates from around the world at the Berlin Congress on World Evangelization. Their real yearning, however, is to reach the new generation of their own people. They do have what it takes. They don't need us to do it for them, and they aren't asking for that. What they want is some technical help so that they can get the job done more efficiently and thoroughly.

Summary: What can we do?

Those of us who come from developed countries often make the assumption that we are superior to people who have less formal education. We also make the mistake of thinking that those who are poor are also inferior. In North America, we are so isolated that we make the additional mistake of thinking that our way of doing things is the best way, that our lifestyle is best, and that our language is best. All of these assumptions are not only wrong, but they work against us in trying to be what God wants us to be.

The high priest and his cohorts in Acts 4 couldn't intimidate Peter and John into halting their preaching after they had healed the cripple. But Abraham and David and most of the other Bible heroes were intimidated at times in their lives, backing down from what God called them to do.

In the same way, many indigenous believers are being intimidated into backing down from what God has called them to do. They are overwhelmed by outsiders' superior technology, formal education, and wealth. They frequently come to the conclusion that they don't have what it takes. But they do! It doesn't come from being able to read markings on paper, from college degrees on a wall, or from their knowledge of world affairs. Instead, it comes from the Holy Spirit, their knowledge of God's Word, and the experience of committing themselves to Him.

In North America, we are so isolated that we make the additional mistake of thinking that our way of doing things is the best way, that our lifestyle is best, and that our language is best. All of these assumptions are not only wrong, but they work against us in trying to be what God wants us to be.

God sent a message to the great King Zerubbabel through an angel in Zechariah 4:6. The angel said, "Not by might nor by power, but by My Spirit, says the Lord of hosts." We tend to think of ourselves as the elite of God's army. Our arrogance frequently gets in the way of our effort to share God's remedy for terminal sin. Jesus taught us that the "poor in spirit are blessed," not the one with the most degrees. Likewise, it is the "gentle who are blessed," not the macho. Those who are full of Bible knowledge and great theology are not automatically blessed, but "those who hunger and thirst for righteousness" are. The righteous will be satisfied—not the one who gives the biggest donation. The "Kingdom of Heaven belongs to those who are persecuted for the sake of righteousness" (Matthew 5).

We don't know much about persecution, but many of our indigenous brothers and sisters do. We need to learn from them because it looks like our turn is coming. We definitely have the biggest bank accounts on earth, but our persecuted relatives in other countries have a big reward coming.

Paul wrote a word of caution to the believers in Rome that is pertinent for believers from the high-tech, developed world. He said, "I say to every man among you not to think more highly of himself than he ought to think; but to think so as to have sound judgment, as God has allotted to each a measure of faith. For just as we have many members in one body and all the members do not have the same function, so we who are many are one body in Christ, and individually members one of another" (Romans 12:3-5).

God has commissioned every one of His followers, and through the Holy Spirit, we all have what it takes. But we can only get the job done if we work together as one body—putting what we have to offer into one pot under the united leadership of Jesus Christ.

Chapter Five

1

Technology—from prejudice to partnership

New tools are needed to blaze new trails in new places!

It was obvious that the woman was very sick. The North American doctor examined her and then gave her his assessment, "You have to have surgery, or you will die."

She took the news calmly. She had known for some time that something was seriously wrong with her body. The doctor asked her to stay to consult with a surgeon who was in the middle of an operation. He was the only one on staff who was qualified to perform her operation.

As soon as the surgery was finished, the surgeon joined the doctor and his patient. When he entered the examining room, the woman stiffened. She turned to the North American doctor and demanded in English, "I want a proper surgeon, not an Indian." Having grown up in a society with a definite class system, she could tell by the surgeon's facial features and hair texture that he was an Indian, the very lowest class in her society. She not only assumed that he could not be a real surgeon but also that he would not be able to understand English, a language spoken only by the educated.

Offended and embarrassed by her bigoted prejudice, the referring doctor informed her on the spot, "You have three choices: fly to the United States for surgery, knowing the trip will be hard on you in your condition, don't have the surgery, or let this fine surgeon do the surgery here."

Technological prejudice

After 150 years of attempting to rid ourselves of the notion that people's worth or intelligence is based on the color of their skin, we find bigotry to be repugnant to our Western sensibilities. The typical North American, however, still has plenty of prejudice. Christians are no exception. Usually, however, we don't realize it. A good example of this is in the area of technology, which is playing a vital role in reaching the world with Christ's message of hope. I have never heard anyone suggest that any technology could not or should not be used in missions. But when the possibility of low-tech believers using those same tools comes up, people openly question the wisdom

> *Is the "you shouldn't have any care until you can have proper care" view of medicine correct?*

and the practicality of even considering it. They even question the low-tech believers' intelligence, as if low-tech was synonymous with low IQ.

When the Waodani believers asked me to help them learn to fix their people's teeth and I was taking in our first "Jules Goldberg" *jungleized* dental equipment, several missionaries and non-Indian Ecuadorians asked who was going to use the equipment. It wasn't my decision, so I told them, "That is up to the Waodani elders to decide."

When it dawned on these skeptics that the idea was to actually use Waodani dentists, they were appalled. "Someone could get hurt," a few cautioned.

"Are you sure this is legal?" others asked.

One woman simply remarked, "They are never going to work on my teeth. I can tell you that much!"

She was right. She had access to professional dentists with years and years of formal education and modern equipment in a nice clean office. But what should our response be to those who don't have what she has? Should we say, "You shouldn't have any care until you can have *proper* care?" Even our own medical system, which is without question the best in the world, no longer practices that. We are being forced to accept that the best care is the best available care.

A good friend's young daughter always wanted to be an Emergency Medical Technician, a goal she achieved before her twentieth birthday. When she began to tell of her experiences in an ambulance service, I was amazed. Here was a teenager being trusted with life-and-death medical situations after little more than a year of training! In fact, I have heard that if EMTs are at an automobile accident and a licensed doctor shows up on the scene, the EMTs are legally in charge. They don't have nearly as much medical training as a doctor, but their training is specific to the tasks they have to perform. We have had to realize that there aren't enough doctors available to ride ambulances, nor would it be financially justifiable, so we have found a workable alternative.

> *After 150 years of attempting to rid ourselves of the notion that people's worth or intelligence is based on the color of their skin, we find bigotry to be repugnant to our Western sensibilities. But the typical North American still has plenty of prejudice.*

If this type of specific education was applied to missions work, indigenous people could perform many functions that we have traditionally thought only missionaries or highly educated national believers could do.

Don't ask the fish.

We high-tech people are so immersed in technology that we no longer see it. We don't even blink when the microwave cooks our popcorn while the dishwasher, dryer, air conditioning, TV, radio, computer, fax, Nintendo, and email are simultaneously going. It's natural, expected, and necessary.

Ravi Zecharias, a Christian philosopher, author, and evangelist, once said that if you want to know about water "don't ask the fish." I have come to the conclusion that if you want to discuss the benefits of technology, don't ask a North American. We are so dependent on technology and so immersed in it that we take it for granted. It has become our "water." We pay little attention to much of it, but we can't live without it.

Remember that it wasn't very long ago that millions of reasonable people in the U.S. and other developed countries were buying huge supplies of dried food, canceling travel plans, building underground shelters, and even stockpiling guns and ammunition. We spent billions of dollars and went to great lengths to prepare, not because we expected an invasion by a hostile neighboring country but because we were worried our computers couldn't handle the date change to the year 2000.

Technology now even forms part of the moral fiber of developed nations. Many years ago you may recall a major electrical blackout that crippled New York City. I was in college at the time and until then had never really considered how dependent we as a nation are on electricity. As the power grids went out, elevators stopped moving, subways stalled, traffic lights quit working, and more. It created a major *and predictable* crisis.

Something else happened that was not quite so predictable. As this technology failed, it took with it a powerful moral deterrent. When the lights went out, patrons in restaurants walked out without paying, taking souvenirs (linens and silverware) with them. In hotel lobbies, normal, everyday citizens (when the lights were on) began to mug other people. On the streets, pedestrians began to break windows and loot stores. Some of the looters who were caught included upstanding citizens who said, "I don't know what came over me. I had never even considered stealing before the lights went out."

And if the power had stayed off, there is absolutely no telling what would have happened. Only a wild imagination could consider all the possibilities.

Technology is critical to getting the job done.

Quite a few years ago I was asked by Mission Aviation Fellowship (MAF) to help them get an air transportation and radio communications operation going in Mali, West Africa. I was not prepared for what I would find, even though I had grown up in a third-world country.

All across northern Africa, just below the Sahara desert, there was a huge band of land where, for reasons only God knows, it quit raining. And when the rain stopped, grasslands dried up, and animals started to die. Famine and famine-related diseases such as cholera began to decimate entire groups of people, hitting nomads like the Tuaregs the hardest. The Tuaregs, desperate to keep what was left of their herds of goats and camels alive, were wandering from water hole to water hole. The animals quickly turned what was left of the water into mud puddles. The people had nothing else to drink, so they drank it too—and died. The contaminated water killed the children and elderly first.

By the time I arrived in Mali, the situation was beyond anything I could comprehend. Aid workers were

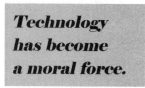
Technology has become a moral force.

actually forced to choose between who would live and who would die. I saw a Red Cross worker count about halfway from the front to the back of a feeding line and then send the late-comers away. I assumed they would come back for the next feeding, but she informed me that they could not be fed. "If we try to keep too many children alive," she bluntly stated, "they will all die, just more slowly."

One woman—a total stranger—handed me her baby and started to walk away! A missionary told me that the stranger had recognized by the epaulets on my shirt that I was a pilot and knew that the only chance for her baby was to send it away from the famine. The mother also knew it was inevitable that she herself was going to die. She couldn't care for her child. I naively informed the aid worker that we would fly powdered milk to this area (near Timbuktu) starting the next day. She informed me that many of the babies were so far gone that they could no longer process milk. "We don't just need food," she said. "We need a way to find those who need the food and the means to get it to them before they are this far gone!"

Soon after I arrived, a message came from the ministry of health in the capital city of Bamako that there was a Cholera epidemic in an area just two hundred miles away. By the time the messenger had ridden his camel to the nearest road and waited for a vehicle to happen along to take him to the capital, days had passed. When medicines were packed in ice and coolers and the return trip had been made, most of the individuals who were ill had already died.

But within weeks, with the use of airplanes and long distance mobile radios, we were able to reduce the response time for similar emergencies from as long as two weeks to as little as two hours. I felt a deep sense of significance in being able to help such helpless people and thanked God for allowing me to play a little part in rescuing a few thousand stoic people through the use of technology. I also felt a bit guilty but was very thankful that my family normally lived in a land where the problems are cholesterol and stress, not cholera and starvation.

Two approaches to technology for natives

Mention technology for missionaries and the question of raising the necessary funds will come up. Bring up the subject of how to adapt these technologies for use by low-tech, indigenous believers, and you will usually get two reactions, one from either end of the spectrum.

#1—The zoo-keeper's approach

This first approach is typical of people like anthropologists who want to keep indigenous people in their natural state. At its best, this approach attempts to keep out all outsiders who have any intentions other than to observe the natives. At its worst, this extreme approach to technology strives to keep all non-natives out and to keep all natives in.

Those who promote this approach want to create human zoos usually so that they can observe and enjoy them. Their motivation is rarely the interests of the individuals in these zoos. I read an article by an anthropologist who went to visit and photograph some Waodani in a village that had only recently been contacted by Christian Waodani. The villagers had just begun to have some interaction with the outside world. The anthropologist was openly critical of all mission activity because it "ruins a lovely and pristine culture." I was sure she wouldn't have thought it was quite as lovely if she had visited right before they stopped spearing all outsiders.

> **Cutting-edge technology to help indigenous people is one thing, but creating technology to be used by indigenous people is an entirely different matter. WHY?**

Included in the article was a picture of the anthropologist with several Waodani in their native dress, consisting only of a "G-string." The anthropologist was fully clothed and smoking a cigarette. In her article she mentioned that she had given the Waodani candy so they would recognize her as a friend.

She didn't seem to know it, but she was unintentionally creating a perception of need and setting an unattainable standard for the Waodani whom she said should be left in their natural state. If she really wanted to leave the Waodani as they were, she should have undressed, left her cigarettes and candy at home, and traded her glasses for contacts. In all reality, she should have stayed away herself. The Waodani are capable of forming quick attachments and might have missed her when she left, not to mention the fact that they surely wanted clothes, cigarettes, and more candy.

As missionaries, our purpose is not to change someone's culture but to offer people an opportunity to adopt a new life with new values and new attitudes. People in Chicago, London, or Paris who come to know Jesus will have the same opportunities. Their lives change too when they become God followers.

Christians seldom adopt a strict zoo-keeper's approach. But when it comes to technology for the natives, whatever bit of zoo-keeper mentality there is quickly becomes evident.

Few disagree that everyone should ideally have access to the benefits of technology to get bad teeth fixed, get an airplane ride to the hospital, get the ability to read the Bible in his or her own language, or get to see the *Jesus* film. The problem is that we feel it is *our* duty to do all these things *for* everyone. The fact is that we can't possibly do all this for everyone—nor should we. Jesus taught us to teach those we reach, to copy what we do, and to teach others (Matthew 28:20) as did Paul (II Timothy 2:2). However, these commands have proven to be an ineffective deterrent. It is almost as if we can't help ourselves.

> **The Waodani understand that choices have consequences. But they should have the same right we do, to choose their future.**

Taking technology to indigenous people seems terrible to some, but those who say this have most likely never felt the frustration and helplessness that indigenous people feel. The indigenous know there are medicines and tools that could save their lives or eliminate their suffering, but they don't have those medicines or tools, nor can they usually get them on their own.

I must admit that I personally hate to see the Waodani way of life change. It is tempting to do nothing to increase the Waodani's technological abilities. After all, I loved the Waodani culture and way of life as it was when I first went to live with them in the early sixties. I didn't have to wear much, and the open-door policy (none of the houses had doors and some had no walls) put everyone at ease. Hunting and fishing were done with spears and blowguns. There was very little tension and no competition. Children went to school in the garden and out in the jungle by mimicking their parents. People slept, talked, ate, and made poison darts and net bags whenever they felt like it. You never had to look for companionship. If a Waodani woke up in the middle of the night and wanted company, he or she would simply start talking until someone in the same house or another house close by woke up and responded. Conversations were not interrupted by the telephone, there were no bills to pay, and there was no pressure to keep up with the Joneses. Everyone wore the same one-size-fits-all uniform, and doing laundry was a snap.

> *I am helping the Waodani change the way they live, not because I want them to change but because they want to change.*

But today I am helping the Waodani change the way they live, not because I want them to change but because they want to change. I've also learned that if someone who loves them won't help them change, someone who doesn't love them will!

The Waodani understand that choices have consequences. But they should have the same right we do to choose the future. Just like us, some of the choices they are making have consequences of which they are not aware. Because I have access to the histories of people groups like them, I try to point out to the Waodani what has happened to other native tribes who have made decisions that the Waodani are now having to make.

They are fascinated with Native Americans and listen thoughtfully as I read and pass on what has happened to these Native Americans as a result of their decisions. If the Waodani want to go down a road that I am convinced is dangerous, I feel I have to tell them what I think and then support their decision as long as it doesn't go against clear biblical principles. If it does that, I show them the Scripture; they are just as capable of following God's trail as I am.

#2—The cloner's approach

The cloner's approach is a much different approach. While a zoo-keeper might say, "Keep outsiders out and natives as they are," a cloner says, "If they want to do the things we do, then they will have to be like us."

By applying this approach to the Waodani, I would be forced to tell them, "If you want to do dental work, you need to go to school and become proper dentists." For Gaba and Nemonta, the two individuals the Waodani elders chose to learn dentistry, that would mean going to at least six years of secondary education followed by five or six more years of university and dental school. That is a possibility for some but not for Gaba and certainly not for Nemonta, who still has children at home and who does not speak Spanish.

Gaba, the son of Tona, the first Waodani martyr, is just as sharp intellectually as his dad was. I taught Gaba everything I knew about drilling and filling teeth in a few days (that is all the training I had). The next time I was with him in the jungle, a young mother with a toothache came a day down the river from Tonampade, a community named for Gaba's father (also the community where my father and aunt are buried). The tooth that was giving her a great deal of pain did not appear to have a cavity. All I could see was a large dark area on the front surface. I probed it to see if it was soft and tacky (a sure sign of decay), but it was hard. While I was gently probing and trying to figure out what the problem was, Gaba, careful not to offend me, reached around with another probe and gave the dark area of the tooth a gentle but substantial flick. The entire front of the tooth disappeared! I realized at that moment that the student had become the teacher.

With all the increased interest and training in dentistry taking place in the village, I must admit that I had no intention of having my students work on my teeth. But one night I broke a molar eating tapir meat with Tementa. It was dark, so I could not fly myself to a "proper" dentist; I did not want to wait for morning. I asked Nemonta to see what she could do.

It was not an extensive procedure, but she did what she could. Since then I have been to two *cowodi* (outsider) dentists for other dental work. They both wondered who fixed my tooth but left it the way it was, saying, "It looks a little unconventional, but it's sound."

As Nemonta worked on my tooth, my concern was not that she didn't have a diploma on the clinic wall. (I'll have to remember to give her one, though there is no clinic wall yet to hang it on.) My concern was not her skill level. What concerned me was the speed control pedal on the prototype dental unit that was sticking. As Nemonta moved the drill in and out of my mouth, it was running fast enough to do some serious body piercing! But she was careful, and I don't wear rings in my lips or nose. I was very thankful for her kind help.

The luxury of global education

In developed countries, we have the luxury of being able to afford a global education. People in developing countries usually don't. If people are going to pull wisdom teeth in a society like ours, for example, they are required to go to twelve years of school, not counting a year or two of kindergarten followed by four years of college, four or five years of dental school, and a year or so of specialization. In all, they would have well over twenty years of formal education. They would know something about history, government, philosophy, Shakespeare, geography, algebra, as well as the sciences, which might be pertinent to pulling teeth.

> *If someone who loves the indigenous people won't help them change, someone who doesn't love them will.*

That is nice, but it isn't necessary. Mincaye and Kimo both have years of experience extracting teeth. And, yes, they do use Novocain—when it is available. Neither one of them has any formal education at all. They can't read marks on paper, they don't have a nice clinic, and they have never heard of laughing gas. But the price is right! What they do and how they do it is appropriate for where they live.

Expanding technological boundaries

When we use technology in planting a church and make no provision for similar tools with which indigenous believers can grow that church, we not only create dependency, but we also trap ourselves into staying longer than is healthy for the emerging church.

After I lived in the Ecuadorian jungle and returned to the U.S., Grandfather Mincaye and our good friend

Tementa were able to visit my home in Florida for my youngest son's high school graduation. They joined me for a short speaking tour on which we visited the headquarters for Wycliffe Bible Translator's technical branch, the Jungle Aviation and Radio Service (JAARS). Tementa and Mincaye both recognized the distinctive planes there as being the same type of planes that once flew in and out of their village.

Mincaye is one of the most outgoing and lovable men I have ever known, but unlike Tementa, Mincaye has never shown any interest in learning to steer a car or to handle the controls of the plane when I have flown him from village to village. When we were given a ride in one of the Helio Courier STOL planes for old times' sake, Mincaye enjoyed the ride but showed no unusual interest. Then a pilot from the Philippines offered us a ride in a JAARS helicopter.

> **They can't read marks on paper, they don't have a nice clinic, and they have never heard of laughing gas; yet Mincaye and Kimo have been extracting teeth for years. Yes, they do use Novocain when it's available.**

Flying a helicopter is to flying a plane what riding a unicycle is to riding a bicycle. When we landed, our pilot, Nard Pugyao, who comes from an indigenous tribe in the Philippines, asked me to ask Mincaye how he liked the ride. This particular helicopter has one wide bench seat for three passengers in the rear of the small cockpit and a single seat for the pilot in front. Mincaye said, "Tell him I see it well. Now I say he should sit back here, and I will be the pidoto."

I thought he was teasing, but by the look on his face, he was as serious as a heart attack. It took me a few minutes and several questions to figure out why old Grandfather Mincaye, who has never shown any interest in such things before, should all of a sudden want to fly the most difficult kind of flying machine.

When Nard gave Mincaye and Tementa a handshake and a hug, it hit me! *Mincaye has spent forty years being astounded by things that foreigners do. He had never seen a Waodani fly a plane, drive a car, or overhaul an engine.* I realized that he had come to assume that those things were too complicated for tribal people like him. Then Nard, a man whom Mincaye saw looked like him, flew us in a helicopter. The light of possibility came on for Mincaye. If Nard could do it, then so could he.

We need not only help indigenous people believe that they can play a meaningful role in the Great Commission, but we need to design appropriate tools and training ideas that will make it possible. Mincaye had no way of knowing that Nard was a very accomplished pilot and instructor with many years of flying experience, but Mincaye's reasoning was accurate. After years of evidence to the contrary, we need to convince Waodani and other people like them that they are capable of doing anything we can do. Then we need to convince Waodani believers to use their God-given abilities in His service.

What makes technology appropriate?

Mincaye would have killed us if he had actually tried to fly that helicopter. It would take him years to learn to fly it and even longer to learn the intricate details of maintaining it. His entire tribe could not afford one, even if all the people pooled all their resources. Seeing Mincaye believe that he could fly a helicopter *because someone who looked like him could* helped me realize how important it is that indigenous people be convinced that they can use the tools that can help them carry out their role in Christ's commission. But it isn't enough for them to *believe they can use such tools;* they actually have to be able to use them.

Technology must be appropriate for the people who are going to use it. The technology used by missions to plant indigenous churches should be usable, maintainable, and affordable to indigenous believers in order for the process of growing those churches to succeed after missionaries leave.

Usable

"Usable" varies from one situation to another, but the rule of thumb should be the simpler the better. *This doesn't reflect poorly on the intelligence of indigenous believers but on the urgency of getting the job done.* When computers were first becoming common, many of us knew that we could master DOS if we had to, but we did not want to invest the necessary time. Then Apple and Microsoft got smart and gave us what we wanted.

> **Technology must be appropriate for the people who are going to use it.**

Now even young children are using computers with ease.

On Tementa's first visit to the U.S., I wanted to see what aptitude he had for operating complex equipment. The elders had told me they wanted me to teach him to fly, so I needed to see what kind of natural aptitude he had. After two short lessons, he was able to drive my car around a vacant housing development by himself, stopping at the stop signs and using the blinkers. It takes most visitors to the jungle longer than that to learn how to climb a tree with a climbing vine.

It would have taken much longer for him to master a car with a standard transmission. To be usable, simpler is better!

Maintainable

To be maintainable, the same simple-is-best approach is definitely the rule. Here, however, consideration also needs to be given to the tools and equipment necessary to do the maintenance. Most new cars are designed so that they can be hooked up

Technology used by missions to plant indigenous churches should be usable, maintainable, and affordable to indigenous believers in order for the process of growing those churches to succeed after missionaries leave.

to a diagnostic computer to reveal what is wrong with them. This feature simplifies diagnosing the car's problem but requires a complex and expensive piece of testing equipment. This is appropriate for a garage in an area with lots of cars needing diagnosis. In a remote area on some mission field, I would much rather have an older car that an average mechanic could diagnose and fix.

Affordable

The affordable criteria are probably the most difficult factors in making high-tech tools appropriate for low-tech applications and operators. This is hard for us to understand because it is difficult for people like ourselves, who typically live on thousands of dollars per month, to imagine what is affordable to an indigenous tribal member whose *annual income might be less than two hundred dollars!* It is made even more difficult by the fact that we so often assume that it is good, kind, generous, and Christian to give indigenous people the tools they need or want. "What could be wrong with giving needy people the tools they need?" people often wonder when I question the long-term wisdom of doing that.

We may be the wealthiest nation and the wealthiest Christians on earth, but that is not a good reason to give someone something. Briefly, here are several reasons why:

- **No Value:** It is much more difficult to appreciate the value of something that costs us nothing. Consequently, it does not last as long.
- **Personal Devaluation:** If people are always given things, they begin to expect the things, thereby negating personal dreams or aspirations of climbing out of their current condition. Always being on the receiving end encourages indigenous believers to see themselves as incompetent, unable to learn even if they did decide they wanted to.
- **Desire becomes Necessity:** Giving a gift to one person can result in everyone else's wanting one as well. Similar but more critical is the possibility that if the first gift proves effective there will suddenly be a legitimate need for many more. And if you cannot give the same tool to everyone, it is better not to give it to anyone. Help make it affordable, and then everyone can buy his or her own.

The best way to avoid these problems and to make the technology affordable, I believe, is to take the money we would have used to *give the technology to a few people* and to invest it in making the technology affordable so that everyone who really needs it can have it. Henry Ford's approach to making automobiles is a good example of this. He invested many times more money getting ready to manufacture a simple car than other companies invested to make much more beautiful and luxurious cars, such as the Packard. The end result was the Model T. He put the automobile within the reach of the average man and in doing so started a transportation revolution. He pushed a new paradigm, and it paid off. We too need a new paradigm in our mission activities. We need a new way of thinking if we are going to have a real chance of carrying out the work that Christ has entrusted to us.

Summary—turning it into reality

Let's invite millions of indigenous Christians out of the stands and back onto the playing field where they belong. The Great Commission is not a spectator sport. We need to check every indigenous church building project to be sure that the mission scaffolding is not inadvertently being permanently attached to the structure. To be efficient and obedient, we need to move the scaffolding as soon as possible, which is almost always sooner than we think. Remember that the Holy Spirit who supervises missionaries in the planting phase of the church is the same Holy Spirit who will supervise indigenous believers in the building, maintaining, and replicating phases.

The message of God's love will spread much faster if we do His will His way. This requires giving the spiritually needy spiritual fish, teaching them to fish so that they can feed others, and then teaching them to teach others to do the same thing (Matthew 28:18-20). It is the cycle of multiplication at work. The Great Commission is a relay race. If we forget to tell believers in developing nations that they are a vital part of the race, *we will end up having to run their part as well as our own.* It would be smart for us to spend more time and resources coaching and preparing our indigenous running partners for the race than we are currently doing. It might mean a little less time preparing for our own run, and it will, no doubt, seem inconvenient sometimes. It might take longer than we want, but it is the only way we can win the race.

Every believer has a lap to run. The objective in missions should be to prepare the team to win, not to put on an exhibition of personal prowess. Paul told the new Christians in Rome that Christ gave them new life when He rose from the dead. Why? So they could produce fruit (Romans 7:4). Jesus put it to His disciples this way:

> *I am the vine, you are the branches, and God the Father is the Gardener. If you plug into me and stay plugged in, you are going to bear a lot of fruit. God, as the Gardener, does two things. First, he prunes the branches that are bearing fruit so that they will produce even more fruit. His other duty is to cut off and throw away branches that aren't bearing fruit. Those branches get burned. My true disciples produce a big harvest that brings glory to my Father.* (John 15:1-8 paraphrased)

By adapting our technology to the needs of indigenous people, we can reach our world for Christ together, a goal that neither of us is able to do by ourselves. We need to keep striving for that goal not only because it is the right thing to do and because we find significance in doing it but also because there are serious consequences, both for those who don't hear and for ourselves if we don't tell. They will miss out, and we will be held accountable for what we could have done (Ezekiel 3:17-19 and 33:2-9).

Chapter Six

Can stone-age people use space-age technology?

You don't have to read and write to fly planes and fix teeth!

One of the reasons why the Waodani asked my family and me to go live with them, I found out later, was to show them how to do things that missionaries and other outsiders had been doing for them. *They wanted to be able to do it for themselves.* To help them in this way would give them a fighting chance of reaching their own tribe with the Good News.

After living with them for almost a year and a half, Ginny helped me realize that the Waodani were beginning to rely on me in an unhealthy way. I kept telling them that I was working *for* them. They had to decide what needed to be done, and then I would try to help them figure out how to do it. But their decisions were often made from clues they thought they were getting from me. I realized it would be best for them if I left. Over the long term I could help them better from a distance with frequent visits than I could if we continued to live with them.

Leaving was the most difficult thing I did for the Waodani. One missionary accused me of quitting, but I wasn't. I was leaving so that the Waodani would realize that the Holy Spirit could guide them as well as He could guide me. The Waodani were scared of being left alone. Among other things, to encourage them I told them what Jesus told His disciples: "It is to your advantage that I go away" (John 16:7). I knew the Holy Spirit was far more capable to direct and help them than I was, but it still hurt to leave.

> *Are we crazy to mix high-tech tools with low-tech people?*
>
> *God did not convince me that we would be successful, but He did convince me through circumstances, the advice of respectable people, and drastic changes in our outlook that we should try.*

We returned to our home in the U.S. to start I-TEC, The Indigenous People's Technology and Education Center, for the Waodani and other indigenous people like them. During that intense year and a half among the Waodani, I saw the needs of the indigenous like I never had before. I wish I had really understood their needs before, but late was certainly better than never. From that moment until this, the challenge has been to bring space-age technology to a stone-age people. The three most important and relevant areas of need include: transportation, communication, and door openers.

If these three areas can be addressed effectively, a whole new world will open to indigenous people.

#1—Transportation

Transportation is a basic building block of development in any community. It is the "go ye into all the world" part of the Great Commission. Because most developing countries lack the resources and technical expertise found in most developed nations, their means of transportation is usually quite different from what we are accustomed to. Where roads exist, land transportation is the overall most efficient and practical means of moving people and cargo. Boats are more cost effective where time is of little importance, where the cargo is heavy, and where waterways exist.

But where roads and rivers are absent, airplanes rule. Vast areas of the world have no navigable rivers or roads. Bush planes, which are able to carry a few passengers or a stretcher patient and which can usually land and take-off in a short distance, are the transportation of choice in such places. The only problem is that such a plane can cost from $100,000 to more than $300,000!

The Cessna 206 is one example. It can carry a pilot plus five passengers. It flies at a respectable speed of 130 miles per hour, and with some special modifications, it can still land and take-off on very short and rugged runways. But indigenous people who live where this type of plane is critically needed don't have that kind of money nor do they usually have anyone qualified to fly such a complex aircraft!

In the Ecuadorian jungle, the airplane is the standard means of transportation. Thanks to the generosity of a fellow missionary, I had the use of a plane while we were living with the Waodani. It was an old plane, but I made about thirteen hundred flights with it in just fourteen months. I carried patients, distributed medicine, and flew the elders to communities that needed them or to where they wanted to teach. I moved people and things between Waodani villages spread over about six thousand square miles of rugged rain forest on the flanks of the Andes Mountains.

Most of the flights were very short, averaging only eight minutes with an adrenaline rush landing and takeoff on either end. But those eight minutes in the air could represent two days on the trail. I have walked between Waodani villages enough to figure that out. At my speed, one minute in our slow, little, old bush plane was equal to two hours on the trail! In four minutes I could fly what I could walk in a grueling day.

A plane of their own

Having a plane *live* in Waodani territory was unique. Planes have always been based outside the jungle in the past. The people figured that if it *slept* with them, it was theirs. As a result, they grew very attached to it. One old warrior figured that if it really was a *Wao-ebo* (meaning wood bee or airplane) then he ought to be able to fly it.

Flying home from his village one day, I had an empty seat and asked if he wanted to visit my children. I said he could be my *co-pidoto* (co-pilot). Cahuaena, a gregarious, old warrior who was once an experienced killer, happily agreed. I began my takeoff roll on the very short runway with a river at one end and a slew full of tree stumps on the other. Just as I reached the abort point, where I would have to decide from the gauges and the feel of the plane whether

> **Planes: The ultimate time savers**
>
> *My dad could make a 45-minute flight into the jungle that once took weeks on mules over muddy trails. African missionaries were able to shave five years of time and work off of their long-range plan in one unreached area when they had access to a plane.*

or not it was going to fly, Cahuaena reached out and grabbed the controls. I pulled the power, and we skidded to a stop just short of the river.

I did a more thorough crew briefing for the next attempt. I told him that the *pidoto* flies first and then the *co-pidoto*. I asked him to sit on his hands and interlace his fingers. When we cleared the nearest ridge, I told him it was his turn, and I sat on my hands. With a mischievous gleam in his eye and with his huge pierced earlobes dancing in the mild turbulence, he reached out and confidently pulled on the control wheel. The plane headed for the clouds overhead, adding a substantial G-force as we accelerated. This created a feeling that Cahuaena had never felt and definitely didn't like. He quickly figured that if pulling is bad, pushing must be good. I knew what was coming, but this was his turn; if he wouldn't mess with mine, I wouldn't mess with his.

As he pushed the yoke forward and we headed for the trees below, high G-forces became no G-forces, and we went virtually weightless. Cahuaena's eyes looked as big as his earlobes. I waited to see what aerobatics he wanted to try next, but he had had enough. Before I could react, he thrust his hands back under his rear and interlaced his fingers, squeezing until circulation was just an arterial dream.

Cahuaena was a safe passenger after that, and the story of his brief tenure as a pilot made the rounds of the cooking fires. No one ever grabbed the controls again, but I was constantly asked to show other passengers how Cahuaena had made his ears fly and his food come up.

"Get us our own plane!"

By the time we returned to the U.S. and had to return our old bush plane to its rightful owner, the Waodani were accustomed to having a plane of their own and didn't want to part with it. They called a big meeting at Nemompade and informed me that they had decided that I would help them get an airplane of their own and that I would teach them to fly it. Without a plane, they said, they couldn't operate their little trading post, their pharmacy, or their clinic. (Anyone sick enough to need a clinic was too sick to carry over extremely rugged jungle trails.) They could no longer visit different villages to teach God's *carvings* without a great deal of planning and a lot of uncertainty.

The Waodani needed a plane, one that didn't require years of flight training to operate or expensive tools for maintenance and one that cost only a few thousand dollars. If it could burn affordable auto fuel too, that would be a big advantage. Finding and modifying such a plane wasn't an easy task, but three years and one false start later, the Waodani can now pilot their own plane for the first time in history; they bought it with their own money!

We began with an airplane we built with the Waodani in the jungles, but I crashed it when a blade of the propeller broke and almost tore the engine out of the plane. It is now flying again, but it proved to be too complex for the Waodani's first step into aviation. Instead, we chose a new type of aircraft called a powered parachute.

A powered parachute is a novel aircraft that looks like an "air boat" with wheels. It is an assortment of aluminum tubes with a propeller in the back, powered by a jet-ski engine with dual ignition and a speed reducer to keep the high-speed engine from turning the prop tips faster than the speed of sound. Depending on how much weight you are carrying, it is off the ground in anywhere from 50 to 150 feet. With a light pilot and no cargo, it climbs like an elevator. We made substantial modifications to it at I-TEC under the supervision of our resident powered-parachute expert, Tim Paulson. We added a cargo pod underneath, a cargo platform behind the pilot that can hold two passengers or one stretcher patient, and additional structure to protect the pilot and passengers in case of a forced landing into jungle trees.

A Waodani plane with a Waodani pilot

It would be impossible to describe what this aviation breakthrough means to the Waodani and their still fledgling church. Movie footage taken by my dad and his four friends on Palm Beach just two days before they were speared shows them trying to demonstrate the need for an airstrip to an Auca man. That was the only Waodani man they would ever meet. His name was Nenquihui, but Dad called him George because he didn't know how to say, "What is your name?" in the Waodani language.

Nenquihui was so fascinated with my dad's little Piper Family Cruiser that he actually climbed into it on his own. When it didn't seem likely that he would get out, Dad took him for a ride. It is probably no coincidence that Tementa, the church elder the Waodani believers told me to teach to fly, is Nenquihui's son.

> **For the Waodani to be able to fly themselves in their own aircraft is equivalent to our being able to beam ourselves from place to place as they do in Star Trek.**

Sadly, Nenquihui was speared by his own people before he ever heard the Gospel.

Having a plane of their own brings an additional element of danger into their lives, but the Waodani believers have accepted that. When we were building the first plane, the director of Christian World News visited and interviewed Tementa. Mission Aviation Fellowship had just had a tragic accident on the edge of the jungle in which three good friends of ours had been killed. Tementa was asked, "Do you understand that you might die flying this airplane?"

Tementa simply responded, "Some of our people fall out of trees and die. Some are bitten by snakes and die. If God says yes, I will die in this plane. I will just go to God's place. But being very careful, if God sees it well, I won't die. If I fly, I might die, but if I don't fly, others will die."

It is a huge step from the Stone Age to the cockpit of a flying machine. The first two missionary planes in the Ecuadorian jungle crashed, and several more have crashed since then, taking precious lives. Will the Waodani have to go through the same costly learning curve? I hope not! We have done everything we know to make it safe. But safety isn't the ultimate objective for us as Christians, nor is living a long life. Our objective is to obey God and to fulfill His plan for us. Jesus said, "If you love Me, you will do what I have told you to do" (John 14:15).

The Waodani are being obedient to the call God has placed on their lives, and through the avenue of modern transportation, they hope to be able to accomplish their goals much more quickly.

#2—Communication

Communication is another must for efficient societal development. Ways of communicating are changing with incredible speed in our high-tech world. It wasn't many years ago that photocopiers and fax machines were state of the art. Today, with satellite phones you can call anyone from anywhere on earth. We send documents from continent to continent at the speed of light and hope that modems will one day be as fast.

I answered the phone at my parents' house in Ocala, Florida, one day and was greeted by someone speaking Wao-tededo ("People" talk, the Waodani language). I recognized the voice of my tribal aunt, Dayuma. Incredulous, I asked her where she was, thinking she must be calling from the capital city of Quito or something.

"Am I not sitting by my fire, cooking Gata [Wooly monkeys] for Come [her husband]?" she asked in response.

"How is it that you are calling me?" I asked.

"Ininamai" (I don't know), she answered honestly.

It turned out that an oil company executive had flown into Dayuma and Come's village by helicopter. Dayuma saw him talking to someone on the satellite phone and told him she wanted to speak to Star, my Aunt Rachel, who was alive at the time and in the *Estados Unidos*. Somehow the man got our number and called us via satellite.

Taking Wao-tededo and other languages to the air waves

When Mincaye and Tementa came up for our first speaking tour together, we were invited to speak on the radio over the Moody Bible Institute radio network. During the rest of our tour, people would come up and tell me to tell Tementa and Mincaye that the people had heard them on the radio. One day, as we were going to our fifth or sixth meeting of the day, Mincaye didn't want to go and said, "Babae, I say let's not go talk to these foreigners. I say, speaking into that little black thing, let the foreigners all over the place hear us, and we'll go eat ice-keem."

Using radio and television, world news can be broadcast to every country on earth in just seconds. The Good News can reach around the world in just the same way. But millions of people don't speak major trade languages. Some of them can pick up radio programs, but they can't understand what is being said. Now that is beginning to change.

A Canadian radio ministry helped us with some radio experiments in the jungle. They gave us some simple recording equipment to try out that the Waodani could use to make half-hour recordings of Scripture reading, singing, testimonies, and community news. The cassette tapes were flown to the edge of the jungle and then driven to the capital city, where radio station HCJB (part of the World Radio Missionary Fellowship) broadcast them on one of their transmitters before the beginning of their regular morning broadcasts.

"They can put a wall around countries, but they can't put a roof over them."

We picked up their signal with little pre-tuned, solar-powered radios made by the Canadian ministry. On the morning of the first broadcast, I was in the little Waodani village of Tiwaeno. It was still dark, and the cooking fires had just been fanned to life to heat our breakfast of banana drink when six o'clock arrived. One of the Waodani men pushed the only button on the radio to the on position. All we heard was static for a couple of minutes until the first rays of the sun reached over the eastern ridges. Then the first broadcast in the Waodani language came to us with those first rays of sunshine.

The Waodani sat motionless and completely quiet (an indication of great emotion). When it was over, one of the old men asked, "Where did that talk come from?" We told him it had come from Quito. "How can those foreigners talk our talk? It sounded like Gaba to me."

We explained that Gaba, from another village, had spoken into a machine, and another machine sent his talk back to us in Tiwaeno. If the Waodani can get a permit from the Ecuadorian government, they might be able to daily speak God's "carvings" to their own people who are working in their gardens or lying in their hammocks. No power lines or batteries are needed, just a little help from their Christian friends, a piece of paper from the government, and God's sun shining on little solar panels.

Broadcasts such as these can effectively reach over both geographic and political boundaries. My stepfather, who was president of WRMF while I was growing up, used to say, "They can put a wall around countries, but they can't put a roof over them."

In fact, in a staunchly Muslim country in West Africa, a missionary with the Gospel Missionary Union is helping indigenous churches set up community radio stations. In what I consider a stroke of genius and excellent stewardship, this missionary got around extremely restrictive government regulations governing private radio stations by seeing to it that the stations belong to the local community.

The mission gives a pocket-sized transmitter and an antenna to the local pastor. (Most pastors are responsible for up to thirty separate villages). The local Christians provide the balance of the equipment, purchased in their local markets, and the station operators. They give their communities sixty percent of the broadcast time for news and local programming. They retain forty percent for evangelism, discipleship, and other programming of spiritual benefit. Those little radio transmitter signals can reach all the villages each pastor is responsible for. Not only does the community government authorize and protect the right to transmit, but they also encourage Muslims, animists, and Christians alike to listen.

The missionary who helped design and set up this growing network of mini-stations told me that there have been some unexpected results. One example is that community theft has almost been eliminated. If someone steals a bicycle, for instance, the owner sends a message to the radio station, and word of the theft goes out by radio; the perpetrator is inevitably caught. Now people of any faith have a good excuse to visit the pastor's home. As a result of these seemingly insignificant mini-stations, there is also something else beginning to return to the people—hope.

Among other technologies that fit under the category of communications at I-TEC are computers, publishing, and video production. It is my hope that we can find or invent ways to make tools in all these areas available to indigenous believers in a form that is useable, maintainable, and affordable.

#3—Door openers

Door openers are technologies or services that break down barriers that hinder the spread of the Gospel to people who live behind spiritual walls—walls that are designed to keep people from knowing what Jesus did for them and the offer He has made to save them. The most effective method of breaking down spiritual bias against Christ's remedy for spiritual hurt is to offer hurting people remedies that work to relieve their physical pain. Religious leaders and cultural traditions can be powerful obstacles to the Gospel. So can the idea that missionaries are being paid by evil individuals in North America to make infidels of the followers of other religions. But a little genuine concern for people's felt needs usually goes a long way toward breaking down such barriers.

Imagine a wealthy stranger with a couple of helpers—of a different race, a different color and a different culture—coming into your community, promoting the worship of a "demon," the reading of strange literature, and the holding of ceremonies at which they eat the "blood and flesh" of their prophet. Would you go, or let your children go?

But what if you heard that these same strangers were medical professionals who could cure cancer, Alzheimer's, and diabetes, and you or someone you dearly loved was dying of one of those diseases? Even if your friends and your pastor strongly recommended against it, you would go if you thought they could save you or your loved one.

Once the stigma initially associated with such people was lost in the miracle of being made well, few would hesitate to accept their help. And if these "devil worshippers" wanted to tell you of a remedy for another fatal malady of a spiritual nature, you would probably listen to them if they had proven capable of healing physical diseases.

Making the lame walk, healing the blind, and curing internal bleeding, among other physical ailments, attracted all types of people to Jesus. When the disciples healed people in Jesus' name and the word got out, powerful religious leaders with political clout hesitated to punish them for fear of how the people would react. Meeting people's felt needs is still an extremely effective way of achieving the credibility that can open the door of their hearts to the Gospel of Jesus Christ.

What is needed to open gates in fortresses controlled by God's enemy is a door-opening tool:

- A "back-packable" Portable Dental Operatory to relieve the chronic teeth problems, which are so common among most indigenous people.
- A solar-powered Portable Video Pack that can be used to evangelize and disciple people who have never heard while the itinerant evangelist-dentist is fixing teeth.

The tool should be combined with

- Strange flying contraptions that almost anyone can learn to fly so that a local believer can deliver an indigenous dentist with evangelistic videos to places beyond electricity and roads—where almost a billion people that God dearly loves still live.
- Solar-powered, mini radio stations that can be heard over small, rugged, self-charging, pre-tuned receivers.

Mix these opportunities together and we begin to see how the whole world could actually be reached much more quickly than it is being reached now. The two keys are allowing indigenous believers to play the leading roles and training and equipping them for their part.

We can do this! It will take effort, ingenuity, and investment capital because it is a big undertaking to design new equipment, field test it, and get it into production. It will take perseverance because we will make some mistakes and will inevitably take a few detours. But we are making substantial progress on some very promising projects and are beginning to see a growing interest in this revived approach to missions.

Comprehending the indigenous high-tech needs

It can be almost impossible for those with formal education living in an affluent society to picture—let alone identify with—the life and challenges of people living under radically different circumstances. The fact is indigenous people have just as difficult a time picturing our lives!

They can hardly imagine places that get so cold that water gets hard, places where people sit at computers making marks all day instead of hunting, a land where every illness seems to have a remedy and every problem a solution, a place with an endless supply of money. Then you bring in technology, and things almost become unreal. Imagine being able to help treat an illness in a thatched hut in the Amazon via a live video camera, talking and asking questions of the tribal doctor, all from behind your medical books at your kitchen table in Chicago. If you had never seen a TV before or witnessed a "live talking head," wouldn't it seem a little surreal? But words cannot adequately describe either world if you are accustomed to only one of them. The "it just doesn't compute" goes both ways.

Words cannot adequately describe either world if you are accustomed to only one of them.

To get a glimpse of a typical need among the Waodani and to see how effectively technology can open the door to the Gospel in new areas, here is an example of what happened not long ago. We received a message by two-way radio late one afternoon calling for the plane to fly to a Waodani village that had no believers (and didn't want any) to help a woman who was dying in childbirth. Some of the people in Nemompade thought it might be a false alarm. But the oldest women urged me to go, and the church elders agreed; so I went to see if I could help the young mother. I had to travel alone because that community's airstrip was short and in bad shape. If there really was an emergency, I wanted to be able to fly the patient to the mission hospital on the edge of the jungle or back home with me for the Waodani health promoters to care for.

I found the new mother bleeding to death from a placenta that would not deliver. She had been bleeding for twenty-four hours following the birth of a beautiful baby boy, her first child. My only training for this situation had occurred earlier when I had acted as interpreter for Waodani women who had asked a visiting female gynecologist some questions, including what to do for a mother who was bleeding after delivering her baby. The doctor had told me to explain that they should massage the mother's breasts to get her lactating and then massage her abdomen while gently pulling on the umbilical chord if it was still attached. "If nothing else works and the mother is going to die," she said as I translated, "just insert your hand into the uterus and gently scrape it with your fingers to dislodge any part of the placenta that is still attached."

There was no question that this young woman was dying. As the villagers stood around helplessly watching her slip away, I felt helpless too and prayed for the mother and her poor husband, who said nothing but had the unmistakable look of stoic agony written all over his face. I had a terrible but almost uncontrollable urge to stand there with them and watch her slip into eternity, but I knew I couldn't give in to the urge to do nothing without paying a terrible price later. In shock, the new mother already had the look of death about her.

Finally, the newborn baby cried, and the mother looked hopelessly and longingly at it. That provided the stimulus I needed. I realized that the little I knew was more than anyone else there knew, so I got a couple of women to massage her breasts as I massaged her abdomen and gently pulled on the umbilical chord. From the smell, I could tell it was already in a state of decay. I had no idea how hard I could pull or how long I should try.

It was too late in the afternoon to make it to the mission hospital before it got dark. Flying after dark in the Ecuadorian jungle is illegal *and* suicidal.

After about fifteen minutes of massaging and praying and wishing I had more medical training, it happened! The placenta finally detached from the uterine wall, propelled by a contraction I believe was brought on by the breast massaging. Semi-coagulated blood exploded all over my legs as I knelt beside the mother's hammock. I thought I had killed her for a minute but was very relieved to realize that the blood had accumulated in her uterus from her previous bleeding.

I remembered the gynecologist had told us to make sure that the entire placenta had delivered, so I asked the Waodani women to check it. I sure hoped it was all there because I had had enough adventure for one day. Leaving instructions to make the mother drink lots of banana drink and water, I ran for the airstrip. I had just enough daylight to make the short flight home.

> *Flying after dark in the Ecuadorian jungle is illegal and suicidal.*

Two days later, on a flight in that same area, I decided to stop in and see how "my patient" was doing. As I taxied back to the end nearest the young couple's house, I saw a solitary figure waiting for me. It was the young mother holding her beautiful baby boy. By the time I shut down, others had arrived. They insisted that I make the young couple tell me what they had named their son.

Waodani babies are usually given the name of a close relative. I was no kin to these people, but they had broken tradition and had called their baby boy Babae after me. The family insisted that I drink banana and manioc drink with them, and they made it clear that whenever I visited their community, I should stay with them.

Saving the young mother's life had been made possible by an old bush plane, a two-way radio, and a fifteen-minute lesson in how to handle complications of childbirth. The door was now open to offer them a free remedy that could cure them in other ways forever. My only regret from that wonderful experience was that I was the pilot and, consequently, the one accepted into the community. It would have been much better for everyone if the one flying the plane and helping the people had been one of the Waodani believers, who could have used the opening to share the Gospel in that community.

If that same opportunity arises tomorrow, maybe Tementa will answer the call in his powered parachute. He is not only capable technically now, but he understands "people talk" and his culture better than I ever could. He is God's man for the job.

Summary: You can't imagine what it is like to live without technology until you live without it.

Technology doesn't seem very spiritual, but then it doesn't sound very business-like either. When I was in the mining business, a friend wanted to send me a document and asked me for our fax number. I told him we didn't have a fax machine because we rarely needed one. He could not believe it. His reply was, "You don't need one because you don't have one. But as soon as you have one, you will wonder that you could ever do business without it." He actually told me to go out and buy one right then, and he offered to pay for it if it didn't pay for itself immediately. Within six months, we had one in our office and one at each of our mines, and I had one at home. Fax machines weren't our business, but they helped us become much more efficient at doing our business.

Similarly, in missions there are tools used often for which we don't even realize the importance: cars, planes, computers, telephones, two-way radios, printing presses, electrical generators, maintenance shops, the Internet, radio stations, pencils, paper, filing cabinets, calculators, and copiers, and the list could go on and on. The irony is that most indigenous believers who don't have these tools don't realize how important they are either. They believe that they aren't capable of using such tools, aren't capable of maintaining them, and can't afford them. The reason they believe this is that usually the people

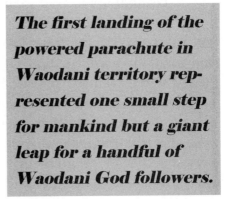

The first landing of the powered parachute in Waodani territory represented one small step for mankind but a giant leap for a handful of Waodani God followers.

seen using these tools believe that the tribal people can't use the tools.

But there are exceptions, like the missionary who asked a little tribal boy what he wanted to do when he grew up. That boy looked at the airplane that had just brought the missionary to his village and replied, "I want to fly an airplane like that." Years later, when the New Testament translation was finished in his language, that little boy had grown to be a man named Nard who flew the mission plane that delivered God's Word to his people. Unfortunately, that is a rare exception.

When Tementa and Galo Ortiz (a young believer and I-TEC student from the edge of the Ecuadorian jungle who is giving Tementa and the Waodani technical support for their powered parachute) first landed the powered parachute in Waodani territory, it represented one small step for mankind but a giant leap for a handful of Waodani God followers. When they landed that crazy mixture of aluminum tubing, rip-stop nylon, and jet-ski engine at Nemompade, it was an emotional event; their dedication service lasted most of the day! It represented huge progress in the Waodani believers' ability to reach their people with the Gospel.

Technology in God's kingdom is not an end in itself. It is a means to the end of carrying Christ's offer of salvation to everyone everywhere. It is an offer He has already paid for. What a tragedy for those who don't know it is theirs for the asking. Almost one billion of the people who need to know live beyond the end of the road. The people who can best reach them are already there. The appropriate tools and training generally are not. But they can be if we work together to design them, produce them, and then train the right people to use them!

Please pray for safety and courage for Tementa and the other Waodani believers as they use technology to help build the church that missions planted amongst them so long ago.

Chapter Seven

Money matters more than you know

Too much can cause greater problems than too little!

"How much money is enough?" I finally asked. I had been building up my nerve to ask a new friend this question for some time. The question was appropriate, at least from my perspective. Admittedly, I had been born and raised in Ecuador and grew up where attitudes toward money were different from those in the U.S. Though I looked like a *gringo* (and was treated as such), I had the rights of an Ecuadorian citizen. I thought I reasoned like a *gringo* as well, but after coming back to North America, I began to realize I wasn't as much a *gringo* as I had thought.

Besides the money issue, the entire mindset is different, as my Spanish teacher in junior high in Ecuador noted. "A big difference between Norte-Americanos and us Sud-Americanos," she explained one day after being told by her students that North America was the best, "es que nosotros trabajamos para vivir pero los Norte-Americanos viven para trabajar!" (We work to live, but North-Americans live to work.)

> *In U.S. thinking: "Too little" is how much you make, "enough" is more than you make, and "too much" never happens.*

Honestly, how much is enough?

When I asked my new friend how much money was enough, I was trying to figure out how much money I should try to make to keep beans and weenies in the cupboard and the utilities turned on in our little apartment. We had just moved from Ecuador to Minnesota—in the middle of winter! I never got a good answer to my question. In fact, I've never gotten a good answer to that question. I finally figured out that it was not a North American question. "We work to live," I reasoned, "so if we know how much money it takes to live, then I will know how much I need to work."

I was beginning to find in North American thinking that *more* is almost always considered *better* when it comes to money. "Too little" is how much you make, "enough" is more than you make, and "too much" never happens. Since that time, I have started and sold several profitable businesses in North America. While doing that, I became a Certified Financial Planner. In all these years, I have only personally known one person who wrestled with the question of "how much is enough" and the equally rare question of "how much is too much."

Money is like medicine.

Concerning money, I have come to the conclusion that it is a lot like a powerful medicine. In all reality, medicine is a poison unless it is taken in just the right doses at precise intervals for a specific period of time. Out in the warm, humid world of the Amazon rain forest, infection is a fact of life. Fortunately, those of us with money and access to a pharmacy can buy antibiotics. In Ecuador you can buy them over the counter, but in many other countries you have to have a prescription. The misuse of antibiotics can allow microorganisms to build up immunity to them, putting everyone, not just the user, at risk. Antibiotics are potent chemicals that can kill the microorganisms that cause infections. Too much of these chemicals, however, can be as dangerous as the microorganisms they are meant to destroy.

One day while we were living in the jungle, an old Waodani woman arrived in Nemompade. She had a very bad infection that had invaded her entire system. We started her on a course of antibiotics that is very effective against the type of infection she had. The day after she arrived, I needed to make a flight to her village and decided to give her a short ride home, saving her days on a rugged, muddy, and sometimes dangerous trail. Before taking her back, I very carefully gave her instructions to take one pill in the *banae* (morning) when the sun wasn't yet over

I can build it myself. Had the Damointado school project been built by outsiders, the Waodani would have gained a small building. But by being contracted to build it themselves, three men earned enough money to build board houses of their own. What's more, Tidi was able to buy a chain saw, which he is still using five years later to help support his family. (It also gives him standing in the tribe.) And Coba is now seen as a builder.

the trees, one at *tekabeka* (noon) when the sun was straight overhead, and another one at *wooyuwootae* (night) when it was dark. I repeated over and over that she needed to do this until all the pills were gone. I emphasized this as thoroughly as I could, and she gave indications that she understood; so I flew her home.

Two days later, word came that she was sick again. The women at Nemompade told me to go get her so that they could take care of her, and when the men agreed, I flew over to pick her up. As I landed at the little airstrip, I was met by a small delegation of Waodani who started to explain that after she took her medicine she got very sick. When I asked to see the medicine she was taking to make sure it was the right kind, they said there was none left. It turned out that she was so concerned that she might lose some of the pills or forget to take them that she took all of them at once! Thankfully, she survived, but it was a good warning to the people about the improper use of medicines and a good lesson to me to be even more careful how I explain things.

Is too much money a problem?

In missions, the improper use of money, like medicine, can create as many problems as it solves. In fact, *too much money is more often the cause of mission failure than too little.* Here are two different scenarios that came from a genuine desire to help those in need; one is true, and the other is hypothetical.

> **Too much money is more often the cause of mission failure than too little.**

Scenario #1: Help me help you.

Two European missionaries (a husband and wife) went to work with a low-tech people group in Papua New Guinea. They had a real burden to translate the Bible into the language of a tribe that had never had the opportunity to accept God's generous offer of eternal life. No one had ever told the tribe that Christ had actually made Himself poor and weak so that He could understand what life in their rugged, evil-spirit-infested, and disease-infested mountain jungle was like.

Almost as soon as the missionaries set up house in the village, the local people discovered that the missionaries had medicine that could heal common diseases such as skin ulcers, malaria, and parasites, all of which made life miserable. People started appearing at the missionaries' house each morning to have their physical needs taken care of by these foreigners with strange white skin and straight hair. At first, these impromptu clinics were a great door opener for spreading the Gospel and getting to know the locals. After a few months, however, so many people were showing up for the daily clinics that there was little time for Bible translation.

The missionaries wrote to their mission leaders asking for help. In response, they received notice that there were no funds to support more missionaries and that the potential medical missionaries were critically needed elsewhere. In desperation, the couple realized that they would have to abandon their translation work or ignore the poor, suffering people waiting outside their house each morning, silently begging for the help that only the foreigners knew how to give.

They agonized over their dilemma and finally came up with a third possibility that involved some risk but seemed better than the two obvious alternatives of either ignoring the physical needs or ignoring the spiritual needs. Most of the physical ailments fell into one of several categories that could each be treated with one medicine. And in the case of the skin ulcers, some simple procedures of draining the affected area and cleaning the infected area of the pig fat and ashes that the people used to cover their skin. The missionaries asked one of the men of the village who had been especially friendly and interested in learning about God if he would help with the morning clinics. They counted out the pills for each treatment into little bottles and then assigned each disease a color that they marked on the respective medicine bottles.

Their clinic helper quickly learned to diagnose the ailments that corresponded to each medicine color and began to distribute the prescriptions very effectively. Before long, he recruited another member of the tribe to distribute the medicine while he diagnosed the ailments and attended to the draining and cleaning of the skin ulcers. Without any formal medical education, these stone-age health promoters were soon holding class each morning to teach their patients how to avoid getting some of the preventable diseases and how to treat others before they required medicines.

As the missionaries began to become proficient in the language, they taught the health promoters how God could heal spiritual diseases, such as demon possession, and how they could avoid other spiritual problems by living the way God wanted them to live. It was natural that as these two men learned about spiritual remedies, they began to include this teaching into their daily clinics.

Scenario #2: Let me help you.

Instead of training native health promoters, who will eventually travel from village to village to train other believers to provide the same physical and spiritual services that they had learned to provide, we foreigners usually decide to take a little different approach.

Among the same New Guinea tribe and with the same burning desire to help those in need, we would typically build a mission station with a hospital and a power plant and a maintenance shop and a school for missionary children. We might even build a guest house, where visiting missionaries could comfortably stay. Around it all we would place a nice chain-link fence to help us feel secure. We might even plant flowers on the inside to make it feel "homey." All of these things we consider necessities.

But the locals on the outside are not accustomed to fences and most likely feel separated and left out, which is an emotion that is not normal for them either.

The benefit of all our hard work, money, and time would be that every person in the surrounding villages would know where to go to get his or her sickness treated. This would probably decrease the infant mortality rates and extend the average life expectancy, not to mention opening up opportunities to share the Gospel with people who come for medical help.

What could be wrong with that?

The debilitating power of money

What do these two different scenarios have to do with money? They have everything to do with money and the debilitating, long-term relationships that often form between missionaries and those they are trying to help.

If the organization that sent the couple in the first scenario had been well-funded, a nurse would probably have been sent to help. Before long they would have probably sent a doctor and other medical personnel. These missionaries would probably have arrived with no training in the tribe's language (because this was a new work and there was no one to teach them) and with very little cultural orientation.

The people of the Niamancoro church in Mali wanted backs on their benches because the people of the Mopti church had backs on their benches. This happened because the work team from the U.S. that built the church in Mopti thought that all church benches needed backs. Fortunately, nobody from Niamancoro noticed the expensive and complicated steeple on top of the Mopti church!

They would no doubt have been very capable of treating the tribe's physical problems, but it would have been a long time before they would have been able to hold spiritual clinics for their patients. They probably would never have achieved the competency of the indigenous health promoters, who can teach their own people in their own language within their own cultural context how to find relief for their terminal spiritual disease.

In the second scenario, the long-term results would probably not be positive like that of the first scenario. After years and years of training the nationals to run this complex mission compound—because the goal has always been to turn it over to them—the sad realization hits: *Though the nationals could learn how to run the operation, they would stand little chance of supporting it.* From gasoline to paint, every item necessary to maintain the compound costs money, something those in the tribe do not have, much less a support structure "back home" that could raise the necessary funds.

Yes, the missionaries could leave, but if they ever cut the purse strings that had long supplied the heavy financial support needed to keep such a complex ministry going, it would surely fold.

Can less funding be a good thing?

The distinction between these two scenarios is that the one with less funding is the one that stands the best chance of surviving long-term. The situation that most of us would have thought was under-funded involved national believers almost from the start. In so doing, the nationals learned how to do what the missionaries were doing and then built on that foundation. In the process of taking care of their own, they earned credibility for themselves and respect for their new faith.

I would predict that it was probably never necessary for the missionaries to turn over responsibility for the local church to national believers because the foreign missionaries never had complete control over it themselves! The nationals always had a part to play, and they simply increased in that role. They began sharing their faith with their patients, they learned administration from running the clinics, and they could possibly have supported themselves as itinerant health promoters. All this came as a result of the missionaries needing native help due to a lack of sufficient funding to meet the need without help.

> **Less can be more.**
>
> **The distinction between these two scenarios is that the one with less funding is the one that stands the best chance of surviving long-term.**

Granted, there are cases where a genuine lack of funding causes ministry to fail, but those cases rarely lack spokesmen. However, the possibility that under-funding can work to the benefit of a mission by forcing it to entrust responsibility to indigenous believers at the earliest possible time is almost never discussed. The promotion of limited funding for missions is as rare as people complaining that they have too much money or employees requesting that their employers give them a cut in pay, but it is an idea that should be considered. The secret is finding the right balance. Like medicine, too little is dangerous, and too much can undo what just enough could have fixed.

How effective are we?

In this century, most missionaries sent from one country to another tend to go from more developed countries to less developed countries. These missionaries are almost always better educated, better equipped, and much wealthier than those they are going to serve. This might seem natural, but in the early Christian church, the missionaries were the same uneducated and untrained men (Acts 4:13) that Jesus chose for His disciples. They were so poor that Peter had to tell a beggar that he didn't have any money to give (Acts 3:6).

> The promotion of limited funding for missions is as rare as people complaining that they have too much money or employees requesting that their employers give them a cut in pay, but it is a reality that should be considered. The secret is finding the right balance.

The rich going to the poor poses an interesting and very serious problem in missions. It is natural for those with more training and greater financial ability to feel superior to those with less, and when we feel superior to others, it is also natural to lord it over them. Apostle Paul, in dealing with the Corinthian church, said he did not lord it over them in regards to their faith but rather "worked with" them for their "joy" (II Corinthians 1:24). His faith was older and much more mature than theirs, but he knew it would not be healthy for him to spend too much time with them. He might lord it over them, and they might learn to see themselves as inferior and incapable of carrying on the work without him, both of which are common tendencies. Paul was telling the believers in Corinth through his words and actions that he was their partner—not their leader, teacher, and authority figure (II Corinthians 1:24).

My experience has been that it is even more difficult to move from potentate to partner in money matters than it is in matters of faith.

The three vital areas of partnership

There are three primary areas that a new body of believers has to develop before they can be weaned from the supporting "milk" provided by outsiders. At the point of weaning, they should be able to

- **Lead others to Christ** (self-propagating).
- **Organize and police their own affairs** (self-governing).
- **Support their own ministry** (self-supporting).

Of these three challenges, becoming self-supporting is usually the biggest hurdle to overcome for most congregations of new believers in developing countries. Sometimes, as in the case of the Waodani in the Ecuadorian jungle, they really don't have anything to give but their time. They have no economy, and there has never been any reasonable market for their time until recently when we started doing Mission Vision Tours together. Now they can at least give their time to help support their church.

At other times, what the missionaries who come to plant a church have—in comparison to what the people among whom it is planted have—is extreme. When great economic inequality exists between the Gospel takers and receivers, the local people can feel so poor that they might think it would be useless for them to give. The way we live as missionaries can create a perception of need among indigenous people, which makes them feel not only poor but also inferior.

The cost of the church facilities and school buildings and seminary campuses we build to meet our own standards can easily exceed the national churches' ability to maintain, much less duplicate. When you add in the sophisticated and expensive medical, dental, printing, transportation, construction, and communication technologies that they see us using, they feel even less capable of helping anyone else. If they can't even afford the tools we have shown them are necessary to get a job done efficiently, then why would they feel they are capable partners in fulfilling Christ's commission to reach the world with His Good News?

What we have is always measured.

Not long ago I had the opportunity to go to a church with some friends in a foreign country. I had met several times with leaders from that church who wanted to send their own young people out into the surrounding countryside as missionaries. They had encouraged their young people to prepare for this ministry by going to Bible school and learning practical skills, such as aviation, teaching, and communications. I was very excited to see that many of their youth were doing just that.

There was only one catch: The church did not have any money to support these young missionaries. As a result, the young people felt betrayed. At first, I didn't understand the basis for their financial inability. Most of the church members dressed nicely, and several of them had businesses of their own. I knew that a number of them had good jobs. "So what's the problem?" I wondered.

After the service, I was invited to the home of one of the church leaders for lunch. His house, I estimated, was probably worth about fifteen to twenty thousand American dollars. The house was very nice by

If indigenous believers can't even afford the tools we have shown them are necessary to get the job done efficiently, then why would they feel they are capable partners in fulfilling Christ's commission to reach the world with His Good News?

local standards, and it had taken them a long time to build; however, I'm sure they had no mortgage on it. They were on the upper end of the economic scale for those in the congregation, but there were others who already owned their own homes.

Later I walked by the church and noticed a number of cars parked out front. Those that stood out I knew belonged to missionaries. One vehicle in particular drew my attention. It was a new, large, special edition sport utility vehicle with all the bells and whistles. In the U.S. it was probably a forty-thousand-dollar vehicle. Purchased in that country, with shipping costs and import duties, it would probably have cost about sixty thousand dollars.

I figured the vehicle was probably a gift from people who wanted to spare no expense to protect their grandchildren in a country where driving habits were erratic by U.S. standards, and the mission probably had exoneration from import taxes. This missionary had probably given up a lucrative career and left a home that was luxurious by comparison to the missionary housing in which he and his family were now living.

But the people in that church had no way of knowing this. What they saw was a family with a car that costs as much as several of their nicest homes—a car that represented more money than their entire church budget for years! It is no wonder that the national members of that church felt, by comparison, that they were too poor to give. They might have felt like the chicken and pig who decided to give the farmer breakfast in bed to show him their appreciation. The chicken suggested they both contribute—and give him bacon and eggs.

Many times, capable but poorer indigenous believers feel that funding for their local ministry should continue to come from rich foreigners for whom it would be an easy offering. They would identify with the pig and state with all honesty that their own giving would be self-sacrifice.

What we can and cannot do

We cannot excuse how we live on the mission field by what we have given up at home. We should not justify technology that is effective if it is too complex or expensive to be used by the people we should be training to take over for us. We must be careful not to violate the scriptural mandate not to "lord it over" (Mark 10:42) our indigenous brothers and sisters economically as well as any other way.

We see many things differently than people in other cultures do, money issues included. But different doesn't mean wrong. Our way of dealing with financial issues will always seem more efficient and appropriate to us because it is our way. To get nationals to do their thing *our* way, we must make them like us. *That* is inappropriate. The objective is to encourage them to be like Christ. We are supposed to be their partners in carrying out the mandate that Christ gave us all.

Money to finance ministry is a real factor in our specialized world, but the assumption that more funding is always better is wrong. The lack of funding can starve ministries, but what often seems like too little funding frequently forces missions to include indigenous believers in the effort to establish new congregations. Doing that facilitates handing

> **Three ways to break financial dependency**
> **1. Design and produce equipment that is both practical and affordable.**
> **2. Limit what we give our indigenous brothers and sisters to only what they really need (not what we would need to make us happy if we were them).**
> **3. Live as much like they do as possible. (This might make it difficult for us to stay very long, which could be a very good safeguard against staying too long).**

off the authority and responsibility for the indigenous church to indigenous believers. That is the way it should be.

It is crucial that we never let superior education, superior technology, or superior financial ability entice us to feel superior nor act arrogantly toward our indigenous brothers and sisters. Arrogance is a powerful tool that the devil has used over and over through the history of the Christian church to divide and debilitate it. We know that "a house divided against itself shall not stand" (Matthew 12:25). If our actions don't line up with what we teach, we can hinder rather than help.

The solution is not to give less to missions. The solution is to give more *wisely* and to use those funds more prudently to carry out our mission of planting indigenous churches that can support themselves. We are unbelievably rich by most of the world's measure. A friend from Timbuctu in West Africa told me that the way my family lives in the U.S. is just what his mother had taught him Paradise would be like.

Summary: So what are we to do about it?

Job 41:11 says that "everything under Heaven" belongs to God, and Deuteronomy 8:18 says that God "gives you the ability to produce wealth." Conventional wisdom says that the way to get ahead is to get up early and stay up late, but Psalm 127:2 suggests that extra effort is useless unless God is involved. In I Corinthians 4:1-2 we are identified as God's stewards; He has entrusted us with His mysteries and the resources to carry out His commission to tell everyone everywhere that sin is killing them and that He has made a free antidote available for them.

We in the United States are living in a rich country, which is the result of God's blessing. But what we have is not ours; we are just stewards who will be held accountable for how we use it to do what God has asked us to do. After much experience, we are beginning to realize that our efforts to build indigenous Christian churches overseas frequently backfire. We end up building our own church in foreign countries, and then we are stuck supporting it forever.

Built to fit our budget and our sense of what is appropriate, these churches are not as important or as attractive to nationals as they could be. They often create a sense of inadequacy and inadvertently entice the local Christians to believe that the best role for them is to be spectators while the wealthy people from overseas do their thing. We could spend the resources God has given us to teach indigenous believers how to be self-propagating, self-governing, and self-support-

> *Indigenous Christians often believe the best role for them is to be spectators while the "professionals" from overseas do their thing.*

ing. After that, they don't really need us. But they never *really* needed us in the first place; they needed Christ.

So how much is enough? Good question. I suggest we keep asking it until we find the answer.

Chapter Eight

Are we on the right road?

We have to do God's will, God's way!

When my wife, Ginny, and I took our family to live in the Ecuadorian jungle with the Waodani, I brought along a chain saw to help them build an airstrip for the new tribal center they wanted to develop. It didn't help with the really tough work of digging out the stumps, but the Waodani loved using it to cut down trees. The chain saw was a novelty at first, and lots of the men wanted to try it. One great guy completely fell in love with it. He liked to put on the helmet with face guard and ear protectors. He would then put on gloves along with a jumpsuit he had acquired while working for an oil company. All dressed up, with the chain saw roaring in his hands, he was the picture of ambition.

His technique, however, was all wrong. No matter how many times anyone explained it to him, he just couldn't bring himself to let the chain saw cut down the tree. He would furiously drive it back and forth like a hand saw. Some of us handle ministry like that. Our role is important, but we just can't believe that God, like the chain saw, does the real work. Jesus told His disciples, "I will build my church, and the Gates of Hades shall not overpower it" (Matthew 16:18).

Do we have the right approach?

In missions, I've found that our method—what we do and how we do it—is just as important as how hard we work at it. Maybe that is why good, old country wisdom says, "If you are on the wrong road, you might just as well slow down and take it easy." To get our method right, we need to frequently stop and take inventory.

While living in West Africa, I learned that to get the right directions, you have to be very careful how you ask for them. One time I stopped my little Peugeot by the side of the road to ask a man how to get to a certain town. "I am on my way to Mopti," I told him. "Can I get there on this road?"

With a big smile and a clear "oui, monsieur" (yes), he sent me on my way. If he had only told me to turn around, I could have gotten to Mopti without going clear around the world!

To make matters more complex, in many foreign countries it is culturally inappropriate to impose your will on someone else. In Latin culture it can even be difficult to get someone to give an opinion on how to do something. "A su gusto" is a common response, which means do whatever makes you happy.

Amongst the Waodani, who are extremely egalitarian with no formal authority structure at all, I have never heard one adult tell another one what to do. Everyone traditionally does what he or she pleases. While rolling huge logs off the runway they were building, for instance, the Waodani men liked to sit and laugh at one poor fellow trying to roll a log by himself.

But God does not intend for us to do His work that way, nor does He want us to adopt an *a su gusto* approach to missions. He has given us various gifts, which are all needed in His service, and He intends for us to work together. To do that, we have to have a strategy that we agree on. We need to be going the same way, and it needs to be the right direction. Fortunately, God has told us not only what to do in the area of missions but also how to do it. He has given us enough direction to be sure that we take the right road. Unfortunately, it has become politically incorrect in our Christian culture to discuss failing mission methods because they might reflect negatively on what another organization or another missionary is doing.

But like my Waodani friend with the chain saw, I need to stop and honestly ask myself, "Is my mission method working as well as it should? Do I have the right approach?" I've had to go so far as to ask myself, "Am I even on the right road?" By asking tough questions, I am not intending to hurt or discourage anyone. Instead, it is my hope that the answers we find will be of benefit. If the job isn't getting done the way we are going about it, then the productive and reasonable thing to do is to find out why.

In search of the right road

Looking at a map is the surest way to make sure we are on the right road. For Christians, it is natural to want to do God's will. We frequently mess up when we forget that to do God's will we must do it His way (follow His pattern), unless it is clear that He has left the method up to us. A good friend of mine says, "Sometimes when God wants to tell us what to do, He sends down a scroll or writes it on the wall. Most of the time, however, He just points out the fence line and tells us to stay in the pasture."

With missions and with the Great Commission, which approach did Christ take? Did He tell us what to do and then expect us to choose our own method? Or did He specify how we should go about accomplishing His commission? I believe that He has been quite specific about the general method He wants all of us to use. Within His overall plan, He may call us to a specific function, but He entrusts us as stewards to figure out the best way to get our specific job done. But even in such cases, we can be sure that God's individual instructions to us will be in sync with the overall plan and method

> *God's specific will or call on your life cannot violate His general intention.*

He gave to His disciples to record for us in the Bible. After all, God's specific will or call on your life cannot violate His general intention.

This truth is ignored much too often without the perpetrator's being challenged. A pastor once informed me that God told him to divorce his wife because she was holding him back in his ministry. I don't know the circumstances of his divorce, but what I do know is that even though God makes some allowance for divorce, it is not His plan. For God to ask a man to violate a covenant that God Himself instituted, in order to enhance that man's effectiveness on God's behalf, does not make sense. That would make God's actions inconsistent with His nature. As a pastor, he must have known what the Bible has to say about divorce, including the fact that God hates divorce (Malachi 2:16). There is little doubt that the man came to the wrong conclusion for his own benefit, not for God's.

The fact is that none of us are here on our own. We should not be doing our own thing like independent contractors. Though this is a temptation that many missionaries have to wrestle with, we are not free to choose our own method. (Because of my entrepreneurial inclinations, this is something I personally have to guard against.) Instead of thinking we can do it all on our own, we need to recognize that we are servants and stewards with the role of accomplishing Jesus Christ's desires and plans.

Paul clarified this when he wrote to the new believers in Corinth, a group not unlike us today. Eugene Petersen in *The Message* describes the Corinthians as "an unruly, hard-drinking, sexually promiscuous bunch of people." Paul told these new believers who were used to doing their own thing that they were "servants of Christ and trustees of His plans and message for the world" (I Corinthians 4:1-2). A servant most certainly cannot do whatever he or she pleases, as Luke 17:7-10 plainly states. Instead, servants do what their master tells them. In essence, we are servants of God, or to put it another way, we are trustees—responsible for carrying out God's will.

Asking for directions

So we are servants and trustees, but what is God's plan for missions? How do you find the right method? Where do you begin? Before attempting to answer these questions, which will help point us down the right missions road, we must first be honest with ourselves about something. Christians have been studying the Bible for centuries and have been coming to conclusions that are so different that it is

Different interpretations lead to different conclusions.

hard for outsiders to believe we are getting these answers from the same book!

Here are five important questions concerning missions that each of us ought to consider.

1. Is what is important to me important to God?

I was painting a man's house during college, and he came out one day and told me that he could tell that I was real religious. I thought he was working up to telling me that he couldn't pay me. Instead, he asked, "What religion are you?"

I told him I was a Christian, but that was not what he was looking for.

"I can see that," he retorted, "I mean, what *religion* are you?"

I honestly didn't know what he was asking, so finally he told me he wanted to know whether I was Baptist or Presbyterian or something like that. I don't remember how the conversation ended, but it was clear that I did not realize how important it was in North America and most other places to join a specific man-made club within the family of God. The truth of the matter is that all those who truly believe in Jesus Christ are really brothers and sisters. We get our instruction for faith and conduct from the same manual, so it should not make any difference which church we attend or which denomination supports a given missionary (I Corinthians 1:10-13). Denominational concerns, when compared to the Great Commission or compared to showing God's love by clothing the naked and feeding the poor, are trivial (James 2:14-16). We need to be sure that what is important to God is what is important to us.

2. Based on good information, did I come up with the wrong conclusion?

It is entirely possible to have good information and come up with the wrong conclusions, like the couple who was flying in an airplane for the first time. They felt a little shudder run through the plane, and the pilot came on the intercom to tell them that there was a small problem with one of the three engines and that it had to be shut down. He assured them not to worry because the plane could fly just fine on two engines. He just told them they would be a little late to their destination.

Not long afterward, they felt a similar shudder, and the pilot came on again. "Ladies and gentlemen," he informed them, "we have just had an extremely rare thing happen, and we have had to shut down a second engine. Don't worry though; this plane can fly just fine on one engine, but our arrival is going to be even later than we told you."

The man looked at his wife and moaned, "If we lose that last engine, we'll be up here all day!"

Good information can lead us to wrong conclusions

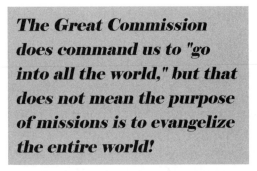

The Great Commission does command us to "go into all the world," but that does not mean the purpose of missions is to evangelize the entire world!

if we aren't careful and sincere, even when it comes to the Bible. It is difficult to believe, for instance, that working hard to meet a valid need could somehow do harm. But that is frequently what happens. If the full ramifications of what we do are not clearly thought out, more harm than good can result.

In missions, it is more important that what we do is productive on the receiving end than that we feel good about it on the sending end.

3. Are missionaries supposed to evangelize the world?

The Great Commission does command us to "go into all the world," but that *does not* mean the purpose of missions is to evangelize the entire world! This perception has negatively affected the method many believers use to carry out their mission. If it were God's plan for missionaries to evangelize the entire world, then we would need sixty to one hundred times more missionaries and that many times more money to support them. That isn't within the realms of possibility—unless God intervenes with a class-A miracle. But if He wanted to do that, I think He would have done so long ago in order to save the millions and millions of His children who have been dying without knowing that He loved them.

No, the purpose of missions is not to evangelize the entire world.

4. What is the purpose of missions?

Evangelizing the world can't be the sole responsibility of missions because the entire Christian church is responsible to evangelize the world. It is numerically impossible for missionaries alone to accomplish the task. The sending of Christians from one place and one people group to another is just one function of Christ's church. If missionaries from the U.S., for example, are responsible for evangelizing all of the Waodani, then what people group are the Waodani supposed to evangelize? They have the same commission that we do.

> *The specific purpose of missions is to plant the church of Christ within every distinct people group on earth. It is then the responsibility of those churches to evangelize the rest of their group.*

Must all evangelism work be cross-cultural, crosslingual, and cross-continental? The answer is clearly *no!*

The specific purpose of missions is to plant the church of Christ within every distinct people group on earth. It is then the responsibility of those local or indigenous churches to evangelize the rest of their group.

5. Did Jesus tell us how?

Did Jesus specifically tell us through the Bible how to reach the entire world with the Gospel? He did say to "go into all the world and preach the good news to all creation" (Mark 16:15) and to "make disciples of all nations, baptizing them in the name of the Father and of the Son and of the Holy Spirit" (Matthew 28:19). What it does not say is that missionaries (people from another people group) have to preach to everyone, nor do missionaries have to disciple everyone who believes.

Who will if missionaries don't? There is another verse hidden behind Matthew 28:19 that doesn't get much air time. In addition to making disciples and baptizing, Jesus added "teaching them to observe all things that I have commanded you." In other words, Jesus was saying, "Explain my offer of forgiveness and eternal life to a few people in every people group. Teach those who believe me and who want to accept my offer how to follow me. Don't stop there; go on to teach them to do the same things—without leaving anything out—that I have told you to do." This includes making His offer to others.

God didn't tell us to feed the entire world "spiritual fish." He told us to distribute the fish and then to tell those who developed an appetite for fish how to get more. Then He told us to teach these new fishermen to give other people fish and to teach others how to fish. As the teaching of others passes down the line, the entire world could be fed, which is our mission in the first place. When Jesus gave the

Great Commission, He was talking to eleven disciples. So either Christ was commissioning just eleven men, or He was commissioning all believers through them. If He had been commissioning just them, that would really have been a "mission impossible"!

But if He was commissioning all believers, then Mincaye, Tementa, Kimo, Dawa and the rest of the Waodani believers have the same commission that you and I do. And so does Nouh ag Infa Yatara, a good and capable friend of mine in Timbuctu. When we recognize that all believers have the same commission, the methods that *add* to God's kingdom are quickly replaced by methods that *multiply* people into the kingdom. Those who say that God is in the multiplication business versus the addition business are absolutely correct. If we don't follow that strategy, the Great Commission will be impossible.

The following little math quiz that many of us learned as kids might be helpful in illustrating the difference between multiplication and addition.

Q: Would you rather have a thousand dollars a day for a month or a penny a day, doubled for the same thirty-one days?

A: It is hard to believe that a penny a day doubled for a month ends up being more than a thousand dollars a day, but it does!

The calculation for the penny-a-day doubled looks like this:

Day 1 = 1 cent	Day 6 = 32	Day 11 = $10.24
Day 2 = 2	Day 7 = 64	Day 12 =$20.48
Day 3 = 4	Day 8 = $1.28	Day 13 = $40.96
Day 4 = 8	Day 9 = $2.56	Day 14 = $81.92
Day 5 = 16	Day 10 = $5.12	Day 15 = $163.84

At the halfway point of the month, we only have $327.67 for multiplication compared with $15,000 for addition. The multiplication method is slow getting started, but it is still the right choice.

This is how the rest of the days multiply out:

Day 16 = $327.68   Day 24 = $83,886.08
Day 17 = $655.36   Day 25 = $167,772.16
Day 18 = $1,310.72   Day 26 = $335,544.32
Day 19 = $2,621.44   Day 27 = $671,088.64
Day 20 = $5,242.88   Day 28 = $1,342,177.28
Day 21 = $10,485.76   Day 29 = $2,684,354.56
Day 22 = $20,971.52   Day 30 = $5,368,709.12
Day 23 = $41,943.04   Day 31 = $10,737,418.24

At the end of the month, if you add these numbers together, you end up with over $21,000,000 for multiplication but only a measly $31,000 for addition! Clearly, over time there is no comparison between addition and multiplication. Multiplication in missions also starts out more slowly than addition, but multiplication will soon overtake addition.

We must teach all new believers to join in the task of reaching the entire world with Christ's offer. **WE DARE NOT OMIT ANYONE!** Sure, at first it would be easier to evangelize and disciple and pastor more people ourselves than it would be to train others to do it with us. But not only is this not God's way; it isn't efficient over the long haul. We cannot afford to send new converts into the stands to watch us do God's will on their playing field.

Asking ourselves tough questions

Can it really be the responsibility of missionaries to act as long-term pastors for indigenous people, giving them the message and then teaching them how to be God followers? Should we be governing their affairs, building their church buildings, caring for their sick and their orphans, schooling their children, and providing their communications and transportation? If we are supposed to be doing all this, then the new believers must be responsible to do the same thing for some other people group. And those, in turn, will have to go someplace else to carry out their God-given responsibility.

Everyone will then have to learn new languages and work in

> *Taking the Gospel to the nations is not a spectator sport, where masses of average believers in the stands watch a few elite professionals on the field.*

a foreign culture. They will have to adapt to new living conditions and new pastimes and new foods. Besides not being scriptural and diverging from what the early church did, it makes little sense. It may be gratifying and feel good, but our purpose is to do God's will, not to feel good.

Learning a new language is hard, and adapting to a new culture and a new way of life can be almost impossible. When Mincaye and Tementa first came to the U.S. with me, Tementa and Mincaye were astounded and confused by almost everything they witnessed. Tementa, who is younger, has had more exposure to the outside world, but almost everything was totally new for Grandfather Mincaye.

When we climbed the ramp to board the airplane, Mincaye was in front. He turned the corner into the main cabin and saw over two hundred passengers sitting down and looking at him. He thought he should greet them, but he didn't know what to say. So he just stood there. I thought there were people in the aisle in front of him, so I patiently waited. When I finally looked around the corner, the passengers were smiling from ear to ear; they were checking out their first stone-age warrior, complete with feather headdress, wild pig-tooth necklace, and balsa earplugs. Mincaye can't speak "foreigner talk," so he was just giving them his million-dollar smile. And they were responding. In the meantime, we were holding up the departure.

During the flight, Mincaye could not believe the plane had a "cooking place" on board. Seeing some of the passengers leaving through a little door in the back of the plane while we were flying at thirty thousand feet over land and ocean made him nervous until I explained that they weren't going outside; that door just led to "a going place" (bathroom).

When we arrived in Miami, he thought the driver of the rental company van had been waiting for me for the entire month I had been in the jungle. How else would he have been sitting there just as we walked out of the terminal? Mincaye loved the grocery store, which he called *caengi onco* (food house). He

> **Reaching the world with God's offer of salvation is not a marathon for a few; it is a relay race that should involve all believers.**

described it in detail to other Waodani when he returned. He explained that "all the foreigners are fat because they don't have to hunt and work in gardens. They just go to this big house full of all kinds of food. You take anything you want, and when you leave, you just stand in front of this young girl. She looks at you and at this strange machine a few times; then she smiles, and you can take all your food home." When I told them that it wasn't quite that simple, Mincaye added, "You have to give the young girl a piece of paper with your name on it, or you have to give her a piece of plastic. But she just gives it back to you."

He also liked the "food houses" where they prepare food and bring it to you. He fell in love with *ice-keem*. Some of the first English words Mincaye learned were "DQ" and "lets eat." Concerning our North American way of life, Mincaye observes:

- Foreigners are always in a big hurry but spend most of their time sitting down.
- Some strangers are very friendly, like the ones that "gave" us food, but most of the other foreigners seem very angry. They won't talk to anyone for very long.
- Foreigners don't like to talk to each other much. Lots of times they drive away from everyone and then talk to them on little things they wear on their belts.
- In airports, when they can't get away from each other, they all sit close but look away from each other and talk into those same little things on their belts.

It would be tough for Mincaye to be a missionary to North America. But imagine what it is like to be a missionary to them—no electricity, no television, no radio, no refrigeration, no air-conditioning, no cars, no roads, no telephones, no computers, no email, no cell phones, no malls (no stores of any kind), no pharmacy, no doctor, no hospital, no gas stations, no fitness centers, and no restaurants.

But there are a lot of plantains, manioc, and some special treats, like big white tree grubs. My dad used to call these grubs "jungle chewing gum, the wriggly kind." You just pop them in your mouth and then quickly decide—to chew or not to chew? It is a decision you want to make instantly because while you are deciding, their fat two-inch bodies are squirming in your mouth. If you bite, you have to consider what happens to all the guts, but if you just swallow, you have to consider how the wriggling might feel until it drowns down there.

Obviously, sending people from one country to another requires ample time for adjustment. It takes a long time and costs a lot of money to raise support, pack up, move, learn a foreign language, get settled, learn how to function in new surroundings, and start becoming productive. One word accurately describes the process: inefficient. How do we justify an average of more than three years of preparation for the typical missionary career that only lasts ten years on the field? We justify it because it is the only way to plant the church in places where it doesn't exist. But when the church is planted, the responsibility for growing it should transfer from missionaries to the local believers. Unfortunately, this rarely happens as soon as it should, and in some cases, it never does.

I don't believe there is any reasonable way to justify foreign missionaries—short-term *or* long-term—doing what national believers could do. Reaching the world with God's offer of salvation is not a marathon for a few; it is a relay race that should involve all believers.

I believe it is only right that we give God's message to people in other countries and then teach them to give it to others. The concept of training and equipping people to fish for themselves also makes good sense in that it makes the task of taking the Gospel to every nation doable. One people group trying to take responsibility for meeting the "spiritual fish" demand for the entire world does not. Sadly, much of our current missionary effort is either intentionally or inadvertently attempting to do just that—take responsibility for the entire world. But by doing so, we are relying on addition to accomplish an exponentially increasing task. We can't get the job done that way, and we shouldn't spend precious time trying.

Re-apply the multiplication approach that the early church missionaries used, and we can get the job done!

Summary—getting on the right road and going in the right direction

In our effort to share the hope for this life and for eternity, let's make sure that we are on the right road and that we are going in the right direction. Let's not try to do what only God can do, and let's not forget that it is only through the power of the Holy Spirit that we can do anything. The Bible is our manual for missions. When our instructions are specific, we need to follow them carefully. When our instructions leave room for our own input, we need to remember what our role is, that of *servants and stewards, not CEOs.* And we must remember that when we carry out our commission from Christ, we are working against the devil's interests. He is

> *I don't believe there is any reasonable way to justify foreign missionaries, short-term or long-term, doing what national believers could do.*

the great liar and deceiver. It should not surprise us that it is so difficult to do God's will God's way. The enemy wants desperately to keep us from doing that because it works against his interests.

All believers are one body with one head, Jesus Christ. We shouldn't divide ourselves by the individual "clubs" we belong to within that one body. We should not divide ourselves by race or culture either, except to allow each member of the family to work where he or she can be most effective. That means that wherever possible, believers should work within their own culture. The exception to this rule is the necessity that the message and the church need to be planted in every people group where it doesn't yet exist. That requires missionaries from another place to go, and it requires many more to train them and equip them and send them.

The purpose of missions is not to evangelize the world. That is the purpose of the entire Christian church. The purpose of missions is to plant the church where it doesn't exist so that it can then evangelize its own world.

Chapter Nine

Making poison has its traditions, just like missions.

Mission methods—
this is not the way it's always been done!

The Waodani love to hunt monkeys. They hunt them for meat but also for a real challenge. (A big Howler or Wooly can weigh up to twenty pounds.) Traditionally, they used nine-foot blowguns with poison-tipped darts. The poison is made from a jungle vine and paralyzes the monkey's muscles. This makes it impossible for the monkey to run and eventually makes it impossible to breathe when its diaphragm is paralyzed.

The quality of the poison determines how fast it works. From the time the hunter successfully shoots the monkey until the time it is paralyzed, it runs from tree to tree, hides, and runs some more. When it is running, the hunter has to chase it, running through the dense and thorny undergrowth on the jungle floor. When the monkey hides, the hunter has to climb high up a tree with his blowgun to shoot it again or at least to get it running again.

It is a lot easier to make good poison than it is to chase monkeys farther and farther into the jungle or to climb more and more trees. This makes good sense.

Potions, traditions, and missions

Every time I take visitors to the jungle and the Waodani men show them how to make poison, the Waodani are very careful to emphasize certain details, such as the importance of keeping the poison off your hands. They tell me that the poison can penetrate the skin and affect the hunter making it. Interestingly, however, meat that has been killed with poison is perfectly safe to eat, and there is no danger in handling the poison once it is on the darts. Another detail that they never leave out is the importance of not eating on the day you make the poison. Now, in most civilized societies, eating is a favorite pastime. Not for the Waodani—for them it is life itself. They would not fast while making poison if it were not absolutely critical. But when I asked them what purpose it served, no one knew. That is just the way it has to be done.

We treat many of our missionary traditions like the Waodani do fasting while making poison. We stick with traditions without knowing why, but it could be that the tradition really is critical. I think the Waodani hunter may concentrate more on doing each procedure just right if he is fasting, or it could have a more direct cause.

After scraping the bark from the vine and packing it into a leaf funnel, the hunter takes water into his mouth and then slowly squirts it into the top of the funnel over the bark shavings. As that water filters slowly through the shavings, it dissolves the poison and then drips out the bottom of the funnel looking like dark coffee. It could be that fasting changes the chemical properties of the hunter's saliva and that the saliva has something important to do with the poison.

Would not knowing why they fast make abandoning the practice make sense?

Many of the traditions in U.S. society in particular are being abandoned with little evaluation given to the role they play in making it the freest and most powerful nation the world has ever had. Abandoning those traditions has led to the need to lock our houses, violence on our streets and in our schools, a rise in divorce, a drop in marriages, rampant promiscuity, a rise in unwed pregnancies, millions of babies being denied the opportunity to live, and an increasing rate of suicide. In missions it would be just as imprudent to abandon traditional methods without evaluating their value.

But what if what we are doing goes against Scripture? What if our understanding of our mission varies from what Jesus' own disciples understood it to be? As a result, what if our methods differ from theirs? And what if we are free to do it the way we have been, but there is a new way to do it that is more efficient? If any of these are the case, then we need to change.

But we cannot abandon traditional missionary methods just for the sake of re-inventing the wheel. My mother used to say "If it ain't broke, don't fix it!" right before I started taking some gizmo apart. But we can't keep doing something the same old way—just because it is a tradition—if it is, in fact, ineffective or even doing harm! We need to find the balance and wisdom to know what to change and what to keep. Perhaps following someone else's example will help us.

One great example—the missionary method of Paul

When we think of the early church and missions, Paul is the obvious missionary to consider. There are three basic characteristics that distinguish the approach we typically use today from his approach. Our approach includes the following:

Missionaries tend to go to one place and stay for a very long time, filling or supervising the critical roles: evangelism, administration, and funding. We work very hard to add as many converts as we can to God's kingdom.

Missionaries tend to stay until indigenous believers meet the same qualifications as the missionaries themselves and have proven that they are as capable of running things as the missionaries are.

An epitaph said, "There you stand where once was I, here I lie where soon you will be, prepare yourself to follow me!"

Scratched underneath someone had written, "To follow you I am not content, until I know which way you went."

We tend to give indigenous people very little real authority and responsibility. We also tend to take back what we have given them at the first sign of failure.

How did Paul do it differently? How long did he stay? What point were the local believers at when he left? What kind of authority and responsibility did he turn over to local believers? By answering these important questions, we will more clearly see what it was that enabled Paul to be so incredibly efficient and successful.

Question 1: How long did Paul stay?

His approach was really quite simple. He would visit an area, enter a synagogue, and preach to the Jews. If they refused to hear what he had to say, he would then speak to the Gentiles. After a time, which could last as little as a few weeks to a couple years at most, Paul would move on to another town, leaving behind a young body of believers that would grow into a thriving church.

In Corinth, Paul trained Aquila and Priscilla, who in turn caught the missionary vision and went with him when he left. Paul then deposited these two new believers in Ephesus while he went on to visit other places (Acts 18:21). Later, when Paul returned to Ephesus, he found there were already new believers there. Aquila and Priscilla had been doing a good job.

Paul continued to travel, making it clear that he would not settle down and become a resident evangelist in any one place. Other circumstances did affect the actual time he spent in each place, and though these different places had different cultures and languages, they were all under Roman rule and, therefore, had some uniformity. To Paul's benefit, he didn't have to translate the Bible; he spoke Aramaic and

> *Paul left the new believers to stand on their own when he knew they were ready, not when he or they felt they were ready.*

Greek, was well studied, and could reason with the best scholars. Also, the Jews and some Greeks knew the Old Testament, which meant they had some background knowledge of what he was preaching.

Most of those who accepted God's offer from Paul, however, were members of other religions, not Jews. He not only had to tell them about Jesus from beginning to end, but then he had to teach them what God expected of them and how to carry it out. Though these new believers needed much training, Paul never became their permanent teacher.

He saw his mission as a relay race and would hand off the baton at the earliest possible moment.

Paul stayed only as long as he felt was absolutely necessary; then he moved on. Acts records just how long he stayed in some places: Philippi for "some days" (16:12, 40), Thessalonica for "three Sabbaths" (17:2, 10), Corinth for "a year and six months" plus "many days" (18:11, 18), Ephesus for "two years" (19:10, 20:1), and Greece for "three months" (20:2, 3).

Question 2: What point were the local believers at when Paul left them?

Paul wrote to the young Christians in the church he had founded in Corinth, "Brothers and sisters, I could not talk to you as I would to spiritual men, but as men of the flesh, as though you were baby Christians. I fed you spiritual milk, not solid food; because you weren't able to handle heavier stuff. You still can't handle it"(I Corinthians 3:1-2). He went on to point out all the spiritually childish things that they were doing. It isn't surprising that the new believers were immature. What is unique about this is that Paul is writing to them instead of being there to tell them in person. I don't know why this didn't occur to me until I was reading these verses in our little jungle house by candlelight with moths and bats flying around my head. At that moment, the light came on, so to speak.

Paul left the new believers to stand on their own when *he knew* they were ready—*not when he or they felt they were ready.* On top of it all, these Corinthian believers were part of a very promiscuous and decadent culture. They had more hurdles to overcome than most new believers do. Paul went off and left them anyway while they were still baby Christians! He called them babies himself, but he left them nonetheless. I have been called irresponsible for teaching tribal people how to fill teeth and fly airplanes. But what about abandoning new believers while they are just babies and their church is just two years old? We aren't talking here about the possibility of causing an infection or getting someone hurt or killed. Paul was jeopardizing the Corinthian's spiritual well being for eternity!

Or was he?

This early missionary, a scholar of the Scriptures and so legalistic that his previous career had been to persecute Christians and get them killed, shows a different side of himself here. Paul recognizes that the Corinthians are saved and sanctified, tells them that they are growing, encourages them by saying they have every gift necessary to be a fully functional church, and then calls them babies.

> *The objective of missions is to plant an indigenous church that is self-propagating, self-governing, and self-supporting. The most spiritually critical thing we can do is to help with the part that is most lacking. If they need jobs, start a business for them; don't build them a church building or a seminary.*

When our children were small, I heard about a husband and wife who were going on vacation. A trusted friend promised to take care of their baby boy while they were gone. They were late to catch a plane because the friend was late in coming, but just in time she called and assured them that she was on her way. She must have lived close by because they left their precious baby in his high chair. When they came back three days later, he was still in his high chair, dehydrated and unconscious—their friend had been in a car accident. I don't know if the story is true, but I can see how it could happen and can imagine the horror and guilt and anger those parents must have felt.

The Corinthians weren't doing much better. They were jealous of each other and were splitting into factions. Reports reached Paul that they were so immoral that they were doing things that the non-Christians would not even do. Paul had taught them not to associate with immoral believers, but instead they were withdrawing from non-believers who they needed to witness to and were maintaining their friendship with believers who were openly sinning—just the opposite of what Paul taught them! They were not only fighting with each other in the church, but they were taking their fights out in public by taking each other to court.

In all their problems and immaturity, why did Paul go off and leave them?

I believe there were two reasons. First, though they were immature believers, there were many other places where no believers existed simply because no one had been there to tell them of Christ's offer. Paul realized he was even more desperately needed in those new places. Second, Paul left early because he realized that it wasn't his responsibility to coach them into maturity. He pointed out that he and Apollos planted and watered, but that God is responsible for making people grow spiritually (I Corinthians 3:6).

I think Paul knew that he could leave when the baby Christians could hold their own "bottles." He didn't leave as soon as they were saved. He stayed until they understood the basics of Christ's teachings. And after he left, he wrote them letters to encourage them or correct them, whichever they needed. He also sent other believers to disciple them. Paul, one of the first and most productive missionaries of the Christian church, the man whose teachings make up much of our New Testament, didn't stay very long and didn't feel that new believers had to be as mature and capable as he was before they could function without him.

> *Good mission method:*
> *Know-Go-Show-Blow*
> *__Know__ God yourself.*
> *__Go__ to where He isn't known.*
> *__Show__ them how to follow God.*
> *__Blow__ - leave to start the process again in another place.*

Whether we feel comfortable with it or not, the approach worked!

Question 3: What kind of authority and responsibility did Paul turn over to the Corinthians?

In Paul's second letter to the fledgling church at Corinth, he responded to accusations that they had made against him. They might have been spiritual babies, but with regard to authority, they were bullies, mean-spirited and rebellious. Paul had told the Corinthian church that he was going to visit them again, but when he didn't, it gave the rabble-rousers an excuse to call him a liar. The reason why he changed his mind is really ironic. Not only did Paul feel he should not stay with a new church for a long time because they were still spiritual babies, but he explained that he didn't dare visit the Corinthians again precisely because they were still so immature! *The contrast with our standard mission procedures today couldn't be greater!*

Paul wasn't just a spiritual mentor to the Corinthians; he was their spiritual father. He said, "Even if you had a whole bunch of spiritual tutors to teach you about Christ, that wouldn't mean that you had many spiritual fathers; in Christ Jesus you have one spiritual father, and that is me" (I Corinthians 4:15). Later, Paul said very clearly, "I call on God to be my witness that the reason I didn't come back to visit, as I had planned, is that it wouldn't be good for you. I didn't come back for your own good! I don't want to lord it over you spiritually. We are partners. You need to stand on your own two spiritual feet" (II Corinthians 1:23-24).

To another young church, the one at Ephesus, Paul not only made it clear that they were in charge of their own affairs, but he explained to the leaders that their authority wasn't his to give, even though he planted the church. He told them, "Be on your guard, not only for yourselves, but for all the flock over which the Holy Spirit has appointed you as overseers; so that you would shepherd them. God purchased them with His blood, but the Holy Spirit has put you in charge" (Acts 20:28).

Considering Paul's approach

When Paul planted a church, he stayed only a short period of time. He stayed just long enough to give them the basics necessary to understand God's plan for them. Then he moved on *because there were so many other places that needed him that had no witness at all and*

> *Missions is the scaffolding that helps build the local church. It is temporary and should never be cemented in place.*

because it wasn't good for them to have him hang around too long. If he had remained in one place, they would have tended to rely on him, and he would have tended to lord it over them. He couldn't leave immediately, but he didn't dare stay too long. He couldn't leave when they were totally helpless, but as soon as they could hold their own bottle, he was gone.

Gone, however, didn't mean forgotten. In addition to praying for them, he kept sending them spiritual care packages in which he encouraged them, rebuked them, and reminded them of their role and of what he knew they could become.

He made it clear that the elders in each church were in charge of their own congregation and were responsible for their own spiritual well being. Jesus said that all authority over Heaven and earth had been given to Him (Matthew 28:18). He told His disciples that it was best for them that He leave so that the Father would send the Holy Spirit to take His place as their Helper (John 14:16-18, 16:7-8). The Holy Spirit, Paul said, then passed His authority and immediate responsibility for individual fellowships of believers on to the local church elders.

The right way to do what Christ told us to do is the way He told us to do it. We have to do God's will God's way. If there is any doubt about what Jesus said to do or if there is a detail missing about how He said to do it, then we should inspect what the missionaries who Jesus personally taught actually did when it was their turn. And if there isn't any clearly defined instruction from Jesus and we can't figure out what to do from the disciples' examples, then we need to rely on the wisdom that the Holy Spirit gives us. It also never hurts to take a look at what has worked best historically.

Summary: What do we know for sure?

Surrounded by so many unknowns, there are a few things that we can be sure of. We already know it isn't the purpose of missions to evangelize the world; that is the purpose of the whole church worldwide. All believers, regardless of how much education they have or how much money they can pull together, have that commission direct from Jesus. One of the necessary functions of the church in order to evangelize the world is to plant churches where churches don't exist. We call that effort missions. This means, by definition, that the purpose of missions is to plant the church.

When all is said and done, the churches that missions plant should be able to grow, flourish, and multiply on their own. When the right planting methods are employed, that happens and can happen very quickly. Along that road, here are a few simple ways to remember the same missionary strategy that Paul implemented:

- Give people a spiritual fish, teach them to fish, and then teach them to teach others to fish.
- Multiplication, not addition, is the only way we can get our commission done.
- Missions is the scaffolding that helps build the local church. It is temporary and should never be cemented in place.
- Know-Go-Show-Blow: *Know* God yourself, *Go* to where He isn't known, *Show* them how to follow God, and then *Blow*—leave to start the process again in another place.
- Don't do anything for believers in another people group that they can and should do for themselves. It is too expensive, there are plenty of other places

that are desperate for help, and it makes the local church dependent—which is frequently fatal.

- The Great Commission is not a spectator sport. No believer should be sitting in the stands watching.
- The objective of missions is to plant an indigenous church that is self-propagating, self-governing, and self-supporting. The most spiritually critical thing we can do is to help with the part that is most lacking. If they need jobs, start a business for them; don't build them a church building or a seminary.
- The Great Commission is like a relay race. Missions runs the first lap. Indigenous believers should take it from there, passing it off to others who come after them.
- Indigenous believers don't need to become like us. They need to become like Jesus, and the Holy Spirit helps them do that.

Chapter Ten

Becoming a hero of the faith

No superstars needed; God uses common men and women of uncommon commitment!

Years ago on *The Tonight Show,* Johnny Carson would do a skit in which he played Carnack, a great wizard. He would be given questions, supposedly of great import, in sealed envelopes. Without opening them, he would hold each envelope up to his head and solemnly give his answer. For instance, while the outcome of the presidential election of 2000 was uncertain, he might have come up with an answer such as "If at first you don't succeed, try, try again and again and again."

While the audience tried to guess what the question was, Carson would make wisecracks and stall. Finally, Carnack the Great would unseal the envelope and read the question that his great intuition had answered, for instance, "How do you count ballots in Florida?"

Asking the right questions

I tend to compare myself to others, a bad habit that I share with most people. If I see musicians or artists at work, I wonder if I could be like them. When I was young and my young friends and I saw the movie *The Great Escape* in which Steve McQueen made a daring escape from prison by jumping a stolen motorcycle over a high fence, we almost killed ourselves trying to duplicate his feat jumping irrigation ditches. The great drama of the bull-fight fascinated me while growing up in South America, but I could not help wondering if I could face such a powerful beast with nothing but a small cape and a sword.

When I committed my life to God, I began to read about the lives of great heroes of the Christian faith. My favorite book on this subject is *From Jerusalem to Irian Jaya, A Biographical History of Christian Missions.* What I like best is that the author, Ruth Tucker, wrote the stories of these great Christian's lives in just a few pages and included some of their "warts" and shortcomings. Knowing that these heroes also had problems and lived in a real world gave me hope.

To those of us who aspire to be used by Him, God has revealed the answer to a question of great importance. He has given us this answer through the lives of our heroes of the faith:

Answer: "It just takes common, ordinary men and women of uncommon commitment. Yes, you could."

As was the case on *The Tonight Show,* the answer doesn't make much sense without the question. But if *you* want to be used by God and have found yourself asking the same question I asked myself for years, this could be *your* answer. If you can't imagine what the question is, the reason is probably that our society and culture have a very different answer to a similar question:

Society's Answer: "You have to be lucky and either talented or beautiful—not likely."

By now you are asking, "What is the question?" The question our society is telling us to ask does not have to do with God or His call on our life:

Society's Question: "What kind of person does it take to gain fame and fortune in our world, and could I possibly achieve it?"

The question I wrestled with for years was one that even the spiritual "Carnacks" of the world frequently can't answer. It is a question that most Christians ponder at least once in awhile:

Question: "What kind of person does it take to become a hero of the faith, and could I possibly become one?"

Each culture gives a different answer. Cultures of the world can be so different that it is hard to believe they could share anything in common.

- In some societies of the world, fat is beautiful, yet our models are thin, even skinny.
- In Africa we saw people groups that revealed only their hands and faces in public out of a sense of modesty, yet the Waodani live totally naked, except for a G-string around their waist; however, they too have a keen sense of modesty.
- In the area around Timbuktu, wealth is measured by how many animals people own, and in other places wealth is still established by the number of cowrie shells someone has; however, in our society, we demonstrate our economic prowess by the car

we drive and the house we live in—both of which are usually owned by the bank.

But there are some characteristics that unite all societies. Most obvious are the basic needs of food, shelter, and clothing, though I have learned from the Waodani that clothing is not absolutely essential. Less obvious, but extremely critical to personal development, is the need for love and acceptance. Without these, it is difficult to find fulfillment.

There is another characteristic need that I have seen in every country I have lived in. After a person's fundamental needs are met, the search for significance in life is one of the most common denominators amongst all people groups. In most societies that we call "civilized" or "developed," fame, leisure time, money, owning more things, and possessing things that are more expensive and more fashionable than others' things are generally believed to help us achieve more significance.

The powerful media and our entertainment system bombard all of us with the same message—that being famous, powerful, and rich can make us happy. Reality states that those who are famous long for privacy, the powerful receive more public scrutiny and criticism, and the rich want more, just like everyone else.

> *We sit under the same indoctrination that everyone else does, and as a result, we have a hard time not believing it!*

everyone else. We know these facts, yet as Christians we sit under the same indoctrination that everyone else does, and as a result, we have a hard time not believing it!

Living in two cultures with opposing values

Life becomes frustrating when you feel caught between two distinct value systems. Welcome to reality! Our materialistic society tells us one thing while the Bible teaches us that the greatest person "is the servant of all," that "the last will actually end up first," and that "the rich end up most miserable." Jesus said that to be His disciples we have to deny ourselves and be ready to die; then we can follow Him (Matthew 16:24). Our society says "wealth is power" and "might makes right." The golden rule has become "he who has the most gold rules." We smile when someone says, "Money isn't everything, but I've never found anything it won't buy." But though we have the highest standard of living, the best medical attention, and more entertainment than we could experience in a lifetime, I see bumper stickers that say, "Life is a bitch, and then you die." Our suicide rate proves that many of us are miserable in the lap of luxury.

On the other hand, I am fascinated by the attitudes of people who have almost everything taken away from them. At the end of the Vietnam War, the North Vietnamese offered some U.S prisoners of war early release as a means of gaining some good press. Unbelievably, men who had been humiliated and starved and tortured for years refused to accept release ahead of other prisoners who had been captured before them. One prisoner explained it like this: "All we had left was life and honor, and we weren't about to give up either one." One of those prisoners had memorized the names of 250 fellow inmates and was encouraged by them to accept early release so that he could give their names to their families and the government. He would not do it until a senior officer in prison gave him a direct order to accept the offer.

In many prisons, men who are deprived of everything they once valued have ended up turning to God. Chuck Colson and several of the Iranian hostages are prime examples. It isn't difficult to believe that material things get in the way of following God when we see the depth of relationship God allows people to have with Him when they are willing to deny themselves what they could have here for what they can have through Him.

Richard Wurmbrand, in his book *Sermons from Solitary Confinement* wrote that the worst day of all his years in a lonely prison was the day they told him he would soon be released. God had become so real and so near to him in prison that he was afraid of losing that when they let him go. God's presence was even more delicious than having freedom and being with his wife and children and having good food and a clean bed. That is incredible!

Work now; play later.

Jim Elliot, who was killed with my dad in the Ecuadorian jungle, coined probably the most famous phrase on this subject. He wrote, "He is no fool who gives what he cannot keep to gain what he cannot lose." That is a great motto, but it becomes difficult to believe when the time comes to put it into practice.

In the investment world, everyone knows that you have to deprive yourself in the short run to gain in the long run. That is the whole reasoning behind savings, 401ks, IRAs, and investing in the stock market. Someday the investments will come back with interest, enough hopefully that you can then buy or do the things you always wanted to buy and do.

An investment into the kingdom of God, however, is not seen with the same degree of wisdom or excitement.

> **"He is no fool who gives what he cannot keep to gain what he cannot lose."**
>
> **Jim Elliot**

And for some reason, when our investment is going to be paid back in Heaven, we call it a "sacrifice." Can you imagine someone saying they "sacrificed" a new house or a nice car years ago for Microsoft stock? No way! They would brag about how much more they are going to get out than what they invested.

Jesus told His disciples that it can be very difficult for a rich person to get into Heaven. Then He taught us about heavenly investments. He said, "No one has left a nice house or given up his brothers and sisters or parents or land, for My sake or the sake of the Gospel that God won't give him or her a great return in this life and eternal life, to boot" (Mark 10:29-30, paraphrased). No one gives to God without getting more in return. We are talking investment here, not sacrifice. Paul told the believers at Corinth that one day the "investment portfolio" of our lives is going to be evaluated for us to see if what we have invested ourselves in was worth while or not. He said that the test is going to be "fire that will test the quality of each man's work" (I Corinthians 3:13).

What we are doing with our lives fits into two categories: things that will and things that won't be burned up in the evaluation by fire, which Paul refers to as "wood, hay, and straw" or "gold, silver, and precious stones" respectively

> **God uses common people of uncommon commitment.**

(v. 12). Christians who don't invest their lives in what lasts will get into Heaven, but it will be by the skin of their teeth (v. 15, paraphrased). If we really believe that we are going to be paid back when we get to Heaven, then this should be the best of all investments because we don't have to consider inflation, wear and tear ("where moth and rust destroy" [Matthew 6:19]), and taxes. In addition, at least for now in the U.S., we get a tax break for investing in ministry.

Of all the investments that pay dividends, there is one investment into the kingdom of God that is by far the least likely to excite investors. It is the ultimate act of dying to self—being a martyr for Christ.

What makes martyrs happy?

Being the son of a martyr, I've been asked several times to write on martyrdom. I have learned a great deal about God's grace from reading about Christian martyrs. Whether they were torn apart by wild animals in a Roman arena, burned at the stake like Polycarp, or beheaded like John and Betty Stam, I have noticed a common thread in many of their stories. They faced the most harrowing, frightening, and gruesome experience of their lives willingly—and in many cases *happily!* Revelation 12:11 tells us that the martyrs "overcame Satan because of the blood of the Lamb and because of the word of their testimony, and they did not love their life even to death."

How is that possible?

A Waodani friend of mine (Tonae), one day told the tribe in a little thatched church on the Tiwaeno River (where Aunt Rachel and Betty Elliot first lived with the Waodani) that God had spoken to him in a dream. God told him to go tell his relatives in the "down-river" half of the tribe how to follow God's trail so that they too would have a chance to one day live in God's place. The Waodani were one tribe divided into two groups by killing vendettas.

Tonae had been kidnapped as a little boy in a spearing raid and had lived for the day when he would be big enough to spear the ones who had raised him because they had also killed his family. But when he started walking God's trail, everything changed. I knew him as a teenager, and he was like a gentle older brother to me. (I was several years younger.) He could make great balsa airplanes and was always willing to take me hunting and fishing.

When Tonae said what God had told him to do, everyone said he was crazy. They reminded him of all the people whom the down-river group had speared to death, and they said, "They will not only spear you, but they will leave your body unburied, to be eaten by animals and vultures" (a fate the Waodani considered much worse than just death).

> **"Wangongui [God] sent me here to speak His carvings; speaking to Him all night, if He sees it well, I will flee. If He sees it well that I stay, then not fleeing I will just die."**

Not only would Tonae not be influenced by reminders that he would probably be speared to death, but he went on to say that God had told him that someone else was to go with him. When he said this, Dyuwi, a sweet Christian who was one of the men who helped kill my dad, confirmed what Tonae had said and announced that he would go with Tonae. So Tonae went down-river. Miraculously, the first group he found included some of his close relatives. They let him live with them and even offered him a girl to marry. Tonae refused because he already had a wife, and God's carvings taught that God prefers a man to have only one wife. This refusal and his teaching that God didn't want the Waodani to kill other Waodani annoyed the down-river group. Tonae called back on the little two-way radio that my aunt had sent with him and said that he thought they were going to spear him.

"Flee for your life tonight when everyone is sleeping," the Waodani insisted.

Tonae's reply went something like this, "Wangongui [God] sent me here to speak His carvings. Speaking to Him all night, if He sees it well, I will flee. If He sees it well that I stay, then not fleeing I will just die."

That was the last call from Tonae. He was speared to death soon after by his own relatives, the people he had been stolen from as a boy.

Many years later when my family and I were living with the Waodani, the elders asked me to fly an old warrior who couldn't walk very well from one village to another. "He is the one who speared Tonae," they informed me matter-of-factly. Our son Shaun was given Tonae's name in memory of Tonae, and Tonae's widow and two grown children lived in the hut next to ours in Nemompade. Tonae knew what was coming but refused to run from it. He made the ultimate investment; only God knows the dividends that his investment will ultimately return.

Common, ordinary, and heroic

What keeps us from being heroes of the faith, besides our fear of having to give up things that we like for a season or some of our personal dreams—and the remote possibility that we might be killed? Usually it is the belief that we don't have what it takes to do anything of significance for God. That is not a disqualification, however, but a sign that we just might be useable. One of the great wrong conclusions in the Christian life is that because God relies on us to make

His offer to the unsaved (Luke 24:47-49), He couldn't actually do it without us. This "God is my co-pilot" mentality demonstrates a dangerous arrogance that the Bible says precedes a fall (Proverbs 16:18).

Only recently have I realized how preposterous it is that God might need us to do anything for Him. Consider the Hubble space telescope. From space it took a picture of the emptiest place in our solar system—to show what a billion-dollar telescope could do—and it revealed thousands of dots of light that appeared to be stars. They were actually entire galaxies! Genesis 1:16 says that God made the sun and the moon, and almost as an afterthought it says, "He made the stars too." If all the stars that we already knew about weren't enough to show God's unfathomable power, now we find out that there are a few billion more!

There is no way a God so awesomely powerful could need us to do anything for Him. I realized God must be relying on us for our good, not for His. But what good does it do us to get an assignment like the Great Commission? The answer lies in the fact that when we are needed, we find significance.

God doesn't need us, but we need Him to need us, and so He does.

One less-than-average hero—William Carey

If you have ever had difficulty believing that God uses common, ordinary men and women of uncommon commitment to become heroes of the faith, just consider the humble, even dismal beginnings of William Carey. This bumbling missionary is known today as the "father of modern missions."

He was not great, nor did he ever want to be great. His big ambition was to be a gardener, but he had allergies and became a shoemaker instead. At age twenty-four he accepted the pastorate of a church that was so small he had to work to support himself. When he decided to offer himself for missions, there was no mission board to send him, his congregation didn't think he should go, his father thought he was mad, and his wife refused to accompany him.

He had all the makings of a real loser. To top it all off, on his first trip to India he didn't even make it out of England due to money problems and lack of a traveling license. When he finally did make it to India, the East India Company didn't like him there and sent him into the interior. His wife was unhappy with their living conditions and with his decision to be a missionary. She finally lost her mind and died, as did their five-year-old son, Peter. After seven long years in Bengal, not one person had accepted the message about God brought by this strange foreigner.

He was also a poor father, who was too timid to even discipline his children. His second marriage so upset the other missionaries that they circulated a petition against it. However, it was a good thing he got married because his children needed a strong hand, and he needed a nurse for his frequent illnesses.

Some of Carey's early translation work was of such poor quality that the director of the mission board scolded him for his misspellings and poor punctuation.

> *One of the great wrong conclusions in the Christian life is that because God relies on us to make His offer to the unsaved, He couldn't actually do it without us.*

The criticism was valid, and Carey even found some of his translation work to be incomprehensible to the local people.

And then came the crowning disappointment: After nineteen years of translation work, all of his manuscripts burned in a warehouse fire. His life work reads like a comedy of errors. His only real redeeming features were a persistent personality, a pleasant demeanor, and a deep commitment to share God's Word with people who were dying without it.

Only God could use a man like Carey to do something significant. If God could do something with this inept and unpolished man, saddled with a malcontent wife, unruly children, and constant disappointments, He could use any of us. And He does. By the time God was done with Carey, he had translated the entire Bible into Bengali, Sanskrit, and Marathi. He translated the New Testament and some other portions of the Bible into a number of other languages, in addition to producing a dictionary and grammar books. And that was just his translation work!

He was also an avid evangelist and planted many indigenous churches. He was instrumental in starting schools and changing heinous Indian practices, such as the burning of widows and the killing of children. On all other matters, however, he showed a high respect for Indian culture and did not try to westernize them. He created several other mission policies that would set the trend in the nineteenth century, which we, by the way, would do well to institute again. His goal was to establish a truly indigenous church that was self-propagating, self-governing, and self-supporting. He gave the Scriptures to the people in their own language and allowed native preachers to build the church.

> **God doesn't need us for His good. He wants us for our good.**

His accomplishments would have been astounding even if he had been an intellectual and administrative giant, which he wasn't. That he could have accomplished so much in the face of devastating opposition, personal disappointment, and unending setbacks, with no computers, email, airplanes, or printing presses almost defies belief. It is believable only because he was committed to serving a God who specializes in working through weak individuals.

A simple formula for successful service

Paul told the Corinthians, "So I wouldn't get a big head, I was given the gift of a handicap to keep me in constant touch with my limitations" (II Corinthians 12:9 [*The Message*]). Paul actually began to see weaknesses, insults, disappointments, persecutions, and difficulties as an advantage because he said, "When I am weak, then God makes me strong" (II Corinthians 12:10).

God regularly uses ordinary men and women of uncommon commitment to accomplish the "impossible." My Aunt Rachel is a prime example of God's using an ordinary woman—one of the most stubborn women I think God ever used—to offer His salvation to a people group who had never heard the Gospel. She is a hero of the faith to me! She began working among the Waodani in the late 50s, soon after they had killed her brother (my father), and continued living with them until she died in 1994 of a cancer that she was too busy to have treated. In our last conversation, knowing that she was about to die, she said to me, "Stevie boy, I was too old by most standards to have ever come to the mission field. I wasn't ever much of a linguist, wasn't much of a preacher or teacher, and couldn't do much for the people medically. Isn't it something that the Lord Jesus would allow me to be of service to Him?"

I asked, "Aunt Rachel, what do you think it was that the Lord saw in you that He could use?"

The secret to being used by God:
- **Love Jesus with all your heart.**
- **Trust Him completely.**
- **Learn to persevere.**

Her answer is a formula for success in God's service. She simply said, "I loved the Lord Jesus with all my heart, and I trusted Him completely."

Then she hesitated and thought for a minute before adding, "And I guess I just learned to persevere."

When the Waodani and I were burying her, Kimo, one of her beloved Waodani friends, gave her a simple but beautiful epitaph: "Teaching us to walk God's trail, Star [her Waodani name] came."

Heroes wanted

Heroes are necessary. We make heroes because we need people to look up to, people who accomplish something of great significance, and we hope, believe, or wish we could do as well as they. A hero is simply a person we want to be like, whose accomplishments we want to copy.

In World War I, very few soldiers wanted to risk their lives flying flimsy, highly flammable, fabric-covered airplanes. As it became clear that this new invention could significantly affect the outcome of the war, the militaries on both sides needed recruits, so they made heroes of some of the early pilots. The term ace came soon after to refer to a pilot who had shot down five or more enemy planes.

They pulled some of the best pilots back from the front lines and held parades in their honor. They especially liked ordinary young men who had found their niche flying for their country. It worked, and thousands of men signed up with hopes that they too would become heroes. The men who fought in the front lines became our heroes, but those who designed these fighting machines and were just as important to the cause received little or no mention at all.

We tend to do the same thing in missions. Most churches dedicate at least some time each year to parade missionaries before the congregation and often have an opportunity for members of the congregation to go experience missions for themselves. But very seldom do you hear of appreciation being given to those who support the front-line missionaries.

Redefining our heroes

Because I am the son, nephew, and brother of missionaries, many assumed that I would certainly be a missionary too. People would frequently come up to me and say, "Are you related to the missionary who was killed by Indians in South America?"

When I would acknowledged that I was, people would frequently ask, "And where are you a missionary?"

But when I explained that I was a businessman, disappointment would often cloud their faces, and they would say, "Oh, I'm so sorry to hear that."

I was too. I was working hard to be a good father and husband. I was active in teaching at church and leading young people who would come over to our house on Wednesday nights. I was also involved in missions, disciplining myself to live below my means so that we would have discretionary funds to help others go into mission work. I *wanted* to be a missionary, and it seemed like the best use of my being bilingual and my feeling comfortable in three distinct cultures. But doors didn't open. It became clear that my aptitude was in business, and that was where God was assigning me to work.

When Aunt Rachel died and some of the Waodani asked me to live with them, people's response changed drastically.

Is it true that you are living with the people who killed your father?" they would ask. When I acknowledged that I was, they frequently added, "Oh, I'm so proud of you!"

But, I was just as certain that I was doing what God wanted me to do when I was in business as I was when I took my family to Ecuador to live with the Waodani. And if I hadn't had business experience, I couldn't have afforded to go to the jungles and wouldn't have been asked to go to Africa before that.

I believe some of the heaviest crowns in Heaven will be worn by hardworking men and women who denied themselves the benefits that society said they deserved, in order to help finance the Great Commission. After all, we can get our reward from men now or from God later (Matthew 6:19-20). Missionaries usually get more recognition than the faithful Christians who support them.

To become a hero, you must first pass a qualifying test:

1. Are you ordinary?

2. Do you love Jesus, and have you accepted His offer of eternal life?

3. Are you willing to trust God with the reins of your life and let Him steer you where He wants to take you?

We shouldn't show preference for any one role in our commission. We should hold everyone in high esteem who is fulfilling God's plan for his or her life and working to fulfill Christ's commission. We should point such individuals out to our children so that our children will grow up wanting to be like them. We must not forget that to reach the world with the God's Word, it will take a combination of going and sending (Romans 10:14-15). Both actions are vitally important, and people in both capacities can be heroes of the faith.

Summary: Can I be a hero of the faith?

To become a hero, you must first pass a qualifying test: Are you ordinary? If so, that is a good start.

Do you love Jesus, and have you accepted His offer of eternal life? That is essential. You have to be part of the family to become a family hero.

Are you willing to trust God with the reins of your life, and let Him steer you where He wants to take you? He's the only one who knows the way, so this only makes sense. If you can persevere and are willing to invest a little now for a future reward, you have all the essential ingredients. Oh yes, it helps if you are naturally weak too (II Corinthians 12:10).

Christ called us to separate ourselves from the pack. Actually, He said we are supposed to stay in the pack but not be part of it (Romans 12:2). We can't belong to Christ's culture and our materialistic one at the same time. That is like straddling a fence. If you lose your footing on either side, you end up in a world of hurt. Trying to straddle the fence is like combining hot water with cold water. The result is obvious: lukewarm water. Jesus told John to tell the church at Laodicea that God would prefer them to be either hot or cold because He couldn't stomach their being lukewarm (Revelation 3:15-16).

God has a plan for the world and a role for each one of us in that plan. We all are searching for significance in life, and this is the only sure way to get it: Find your place in God's plan. Too many of us want to make our plans to serve God and then beg Him to come help us when we can't handle things by ourselves. God isn't looking for a co-pilot's job. He is in the front seat and is offering us positions as His crew.

Actually, God is always looking for crew for all positions. No experience is necessary. Company policy is to have one of the veterans train new recruits. As soon as they have the basics down, they start training others. That way the enterprise can expand almost without limit. *One position may be more visible than another, but every position is just as important and offers the same benefits.* Everyone who faithfully carries the load assigned to him or her gets full benefits now, a free ticket, and stock in the company when his or her part is complete.

If you want to be a hero of the faith, it is vitally important that you remember this: Becoming a hero is not dependent on who you are. It is dependent on what you let God do with you (your mission), on why you do it (your motive), and on whom you do it for (your master). You *can* be a hero of the faith!

Epilogue

Stone-age warrior speaks out on world evangelism.

In the summer of 2000, the Billy Graham organization sponsored Amsterdam 2000, a conference for evangelists from all over the world. Tementa, Mincaye, and I were invited to attend and to take part. Actually, we were to have two very small parts: to give a testimony just before Chuck Colson gave a plenary address one evening and to do a workshop.

The testimony, I think, was just intended to add a little color to this major evangelistic event. The purpose of the workshop was to demonstrate some of the unique tools that are being developed at I-TEC (the Indigenous People's Technology and Education Center), a non-profit organization started at the Waodani's prompting. These tools are designed to help make it possible for national believers to take a hand-off from missions in the relay race to get God's message to everyone on the face of the earth.

There is much about the world that Tementa and Mincaye don't understand. Tementa wonders how foreigners get so fat eating so much grass and leaves (salads). Mincaye wonders why foreigners spend so much time looking for little white things on golf courses if they are too hard to eat.

We almost didn't go because my only daughter, Stephenie, had died unexpectedly just a few days before we were to leave. Tementa and Mincaye couldn't go without me due to the language and cultural barriers, and as members of our family, they were grieving too. But my family decided we should not take the chance that our loss might benefit the devil's plans to keep us away from this conference, so we went.

> **A Dream Fulfilled**
> *While this book was being written, the first Waodani aircraft in history made its maiden flights over Waodani territory with a Waodani at the controls.*

The conference was already in session when we arrived in the Netherlands. When we walked into the huge arena, it was packed with people of every size, shape, and color on the planet. It turned out that there were delegates from 209 different nations, more countries than even the United Nations has ever assembled in one place at the same time. There were more dark faces than light ones, which really intrigued Mincaye.

Old Grandfather Mincaye is definitely a people person. He loves meeting new people, smiles easily, and communicates with everyone whether he speaks the language or not. In that first meeting, we were asked to divide into small groups to pray for the conference and for each other. We were sitting behind some delegates from Mozambique and were going to pray with them; first, however, they wanted to know where Tementa and Mincaye were from, and Mincaye and Tementa wanted to know about them.

The Waodani call all non-Waodani, *cowodi*. The connotation is that if you are not Wao, you are not a "true person" and only relatively human. The Waodani have explained to me that white-skinned people are especially suspect. (They always try to assure me that I am not included.) *Cowodi* look like bugs that live in dead trees, white from living in the dark.

Well, if white skin is weak in comparison to their beautiful bronze complexions, then what about black skin? I just knew that Mincaye wanted to feel these men's skin, the part not covered by their flowing robes. His feather headdress, pig tooth necklace, and balsa plugs in the large holes in his ears intrigued them, but I was pretty sure they wouldn't understand what was going on if he started petting one of them while we prayed. Fortunately, Mincaye restrained himself.

Although we normally stand out in a crowd, the three of us blended in quite well at the conference. When I explained to Tementa and Mincaye that everyone of the thousands of people in attendance was a "God follower" who had came from countries all over the "dirt" (world) to share and learn ideas for taking God's "carvings" (the Bible) to other people, they were obviously excited. The second day we were there we were supposed to share our testimonies. We had only been allocated ten minutes. That was not much time to introduce ourselves and for three of us to tell what God has done in our lives, especially when I would have to translate for Tementa and Mincaye. We decided that I would introduce Tementa and Mincaye; then we would let Mincaye speak, and I would translate for him.

There were only a couple of problems. We were told that all speakers had to write out what they were going to say so that they would stay on topic and so that they would be kept on schedule. Mincaye couldn't write what he was going to say, and he couldn't read it even if someone else wrote it for him. Worse yet, he doesn't know what ten minutes is and doesn't think much of schedules. I wondered too what would happen when he and Tementa found themselves standing in front of seven times as many people as they have in their entire tribe.

On the platform that night, Tementa and Mincaye were dressed up for the occasion. Many nationals at the conference were wearing their traditional dress, but a G-string didn't seem right for the occasion, so Tementa and Mincaye opted for sleeveless black t-shirts, khaki pants, headdresses, and other tribal ornamentation, as well as spears and a blowgun.

When it was our turn, we made our way to the front of the platform as a short introductory video was shown. When the spotlights came on, Tementa and Mincaye maintained their composure. I started out by introducing Tementa as a tribal elder and mentioned that his father was a stone-age warrior whom my father had taken for his first and only airplane ride before they were both speared in separate incidents. I told the audience that the tribal believers had asked me to teach Tementa to fly so that he could take them from village to village to evangelize and disciple their own people. I finished his introduction by telling them that just days before Amsterdam 2000, Tementa flew an aircraft by himself, the first person in history from his tribe to ever do so.

The auditorium erupted in applause. Tementa didn't know what I was saying, and he didn't know that they were applauding for him or why. It was as though the thousands of delegates suddenly had the same thought at the very same time: "If this little man standing in front of us with a feather headdress and a spear can fly an airplane, then we can too. And if we can fly airplanes, there isn't anything that can keep us from reaching everyone in the world with God's Good News."

Next, I introduced Mincaye as a grandfather to my children, who was also mourning the loss of his only blond granddaughter, whom we both loved very much. I told the delegates that Mincaye had killed my children's own grandfather before he learned to walk "God's trail." Then I turned it over to Mincaye.

I didn't know what he would say or how he would say it, and because Mincaye is always animated and usually speaks very fast, I had to be careful how I translated; everything I translated into English was being simultaneously translated into twenty-eight major foreign languages spoken by the delegates. Mincaye was eloquent! He explained how he lived "badly, badly, hating and killing, that is how I lived" before he started walking God's trail. Then he went on to briefly explain how much better life was since he started following God and how he wanted to tell the rest of his people how to follow God too.

I couldn't see my watch, but I figured we were out of time. There was one more thing I wanted to do. I gave Mincaye our usual clue that it was time to end. "Idaewaa?" I asked, meaning, "Is it enough?"

But he answered, "Ayae" (more). He went right on, "Now I see you God followers from all over the world very well. Leaving here and going back to our own places, I will still see you again when we live together in God's place." The audience broke out in another prolonged applause as they had already done several times. Then he concluded. He didn't know that all these thousands of people in front of him were evangelists; I hadn't told him because I don't know a word for evangelist in his language. Mincaye just assumed that if they were God followers then they would be telling people how to walk "God's trail." He finished by saying, "Now I say to all of you, each of us going to our own place, we should speak God's carving very clearly so that going to God's place we will take many people with us!"

When the applause died down, I asked the delegates to help me give a message to my two dear brothers in Christ, faithful Tementa and old Grandfather Mincaye. The idea had come from a friend who is helping in the making of a movie about the Waodani (Auca) story. I asked the delegates from 209 nations who had heard what is often called "The Auca Story" and whose lives had been impacted by it if they would stand for just a minute. I know that God has used this story to positively influence many people all over the world, and I expected a small percentage of delegates to stand. I wanted to be able to explain later to Tementa and Mincaye that the delegates had stood as a testimony to the fact that God can use anyone to give life, including even an old warrior whose intent was to kill.

As soon as the words were out of my mouth, with just an instant for the translators to transmit the words to the delegates in their own languages via earphone radios, *almost the entire auditorium stood to its feet!* It was the most humbling and gratifying demonstration of God's sovereignty that I have ever witnessed.

I have heard from those in charge of the conference and from delegates of many countries that Mincaye's testimony, squeezed in between numerous great speakers, was one of the most memorable and profound addresses at Amsterdam 2000.

If God can use an illiterate old warrior from the wilds of the Amazon to inspire evangelists from all over the world, then He can use you and me to reach three billion children whom He loves and wants for His own. But if Mincaye can speak to twelve thousand evangelists from all over the world, why can't he speak to his own people who number eighteen hundred?

The answer lies in the fact that there were planes, cars, radios, computers, and money to help him get to Amsterdam, but he hasn't had these same tools to get God's message to the twenty-three scattered villages where his people live.

I explained in our workshop why the lack of appropriate technology was a major hindrance, keeping high-tech missionaries from being able to hand off their responsibility and authority to local believers, who then grow the churches that missionaries planted. I explained what we are doing to help solve that problem as Tementa and Mincaye demonstrated some of their new equipment and skills.

They set up an I-TEC portable dental operatory and asked for a volunteer patient from the audience. When a young lady came forward, they put her in the portable dental chair. Tementa picked up the electric drill, but first Mincaye had to give her anesthesia. The audience didn't know that Mincaye is a great natural actor. He took a huge syringe and proceeded to act as though he were giving the young lady shots of Novocain. The audience thought he was really doing it until Mincaye looked up with a big grin on his face, and then they realized he was just pretending.

Next, Tementa demonstrated Waodani technology. We had taken a nine-foot blowgun with us, and one of the conference stewards had bought us some helium-filled "monkeys." I was hoping for regular balloons, which explode when they are hit by poison-tip darts. Unfortunately, we were given mylar balloons, which leak when they are shot but don't explode.

The balloons were on long strings, floating just under the high ceiling of the auditorium on one end of the stage. Tementa backed all the way up to the opposite side and deftly shot at one balloon that the audience had chosen. When Tementa shot, I knew the dart had gone right through the balloon because I know Tementa's skill as a hunter. I realized, however, that the audience would have its doubts. I told of other demonstrations we had done in other places, trying to convince them of his prowess. As I was speaking, the audience members all looked up and drew in their breath at the same time. The balloon that they had picked for Tementa to shoot was drifting slowly down to the floor.

We showed a video of the Waodani doing dental work, the Waodani showing the *Jesus* film on an inexpensive I-TEC portable video pack to other Waodani, and Tementa's solo flight in a powered parachute. We talked about other technology, such as inexpensive computers, printing equipment, solar-powered radio transmitters and receivers, and other tools that indigenous believers need. Getting these tools will free missionaries in their countries to move on to the eight thousand people groups that still have no witness and desperately need those missionaries.

After our session, everywhere we went in Amsterdam we were swarmed by delegates from other countries who wanted to meet Tementa and Mincaye and have pictures taken with them. Some of the people were from countries I had never heard of. I could not find many of their homes on a map, but all of them had one thing in common: a desire to follow "God's trail" and to tell others so that others can follow Him too. Some were well educated; some were not. Some were very poor while others were fairly well off. There were young and old, men and women. They spoke many languages and saw the world through the filters of widely disparate cultures.

Tementa, Mincaye, and I came away from that great conference with one indelible realization. God can use anyone. He is looking for common, ordinary men and women of uncommon commitment. He can use you too, and He will if you let Him. It is an adventure you shouldn't miss!

I-TEC CONTACT INFORMATION

For more information on the Indigenous People's Technology and Education Center or Steve Saint, please contact I-TEC at

www.i-tecusa.org

i-tec@i-tecusa.org

I-TEC, Inc.
10575 SW 147th Circle
Dunnellon, FL 34432

352-465-4545

I-TEC is a charitable organization and is supported by gifts that are tax deductible. Proceeds from this book go toward advancing the Gospel.

To Order The Great Omission

Visit the I-TEC web page and fill out the order form, or contact YWAM Publishing at www.ywampublishing.com.

To Receive the I-TEC Newsletter

Visit the I-TEC web page and fill out your e-mail information on the form provided, or e-mail your information (name, e-mail address, and telephone number) to the address above and write "The I-TEC Newsletter" in the subject line.

Why train and equip indigenous Christians when we can do it for them?

We can't do it for them! And we shouldn't, even if we could. Our mandate is to take what we have been taught and teach others to teach others (Matthew 28:20).

Paul said, "And the things which you have heard from me...these entrust to faithful men, who will be able to teach others also" (II Timothy 2:2). Jesus didn't say, "Follow me and I will give you fish." Instead, He took a bunch of common, mostly uneducated men and made them "fishers of men" (Matthew 4:19). Now he has commissioned us to do the same.

Fishers of men need training and "tackle," which consists of **door openers** like I-TEC's Portable Dental System. Using I-TEC's video-based Non-Verbal Training System, we can actually train people who cannot read how to drill and fill teeth. The Waodani said, "If we can fix their hurting teeth, they will see us well, and we will teach them how God can fix their hearts so they can live forever."

Multipliers are tools that multiply effort and reduce time. I-TEC's fiberglass planing canoe, parachute plane, and Portable Video System fit into this category.

Our great omission in carrying out Christ's Great Commission is leaving national believers out of the game plan.

I-TEC is developing innovative tools and training systems that help national believers carry the Gospel to people everywhere. I-TEC teaches missionaries and indigenous God Followers how to use these tools and how to train others to use them.